STRANGE THINGS IN THE WOODS

A COLLECTION OF TERRIFYING TALES

STEVE STOCKTON

BEYOND THE FRAY

Publishing

ISBN 13: 978-1-7344198-1-8

Beyond The Fray Publishing, a division of Beyond The Fray, LLC, San Diego, CA

www.beyondthefraypublishing.com

BEYOND THE FRAY

Publishing

INTRODUCTION

All my life, I've been fascinated with the woods. While it's marvelous to be surrounded by nature, there is also at times a certain 'creep factor' involved. As anyone who has spent a considerable amount of time in the great outdoors will tell you, there are some places in the woods that just don't feel right, for lack of a better word. Also, by the same turn, there are weird things to be found in the woods, many of which truly defy any rational explanation.

As a youth, I grew up on a small farm in East Tennessee, not far from Knoxville and Oak Ridge. While not considered deep woods by any stretch of the imagination, we had several acres that were heavily wooded with old-growth timber. Factor in that our property also bordered vast, undeveloped land claimed by the Tennessee Valley Authority (TVA), and you have the perfect recipe for youthful adventure and exploration.

Blessed with an active imagination and a love for adventure, these woods were full of countless hours of time spent looking for anything weird or out of the ordinary. As I grew older, my forays into the woods expanded, and I've had the opportunity to explore many national parks and forests. I sometimes saw strange things that defy explanation (my own personal experiences are currently being compiled for publication in a separate volume).

Due to my own experiences in the great outdoors, I also began talking to family and friends, mostly older folks, and collecting stories of strange things they had encountered in the woods—this book is a culmination of those conversations.

Many of the tellers of these tales have passed on, but their stories continue to live in my imagination and now in the printed word. Where possible, I've left the language and 'mountain slang' intact just as it was related to me, to give the true feel of the story—whether you call a place a 'hollow' or a 'holler' makes no difference, as long as we understand each other.

I hope you enjoy reading these stories as much as I enjoyed collecting them over the years. If you yourself have ever encountered anything weird in the woods, I'd love to hear from you; my email address can be found at the end of the book.

– Steve, September 2013.

CHAPTER 1

THE FLYING ORGAN

I grew up on a several-hundred-acre farm in Jamestown, Tennessee, near what is now the Big South Fork National Park. My older brother, Leonard, and I were just kids, so this would have placed the event sometime in the early 1930s.

We were down by one of the creeks on our property, about a half mile or so from our family's farmhouse. We lived in a very remote and rugged area of the Cumberland Plateau, and our 'nearest' neighbor was several miles away. It was summertime, getting close to twilight, and we were cooling our feet in the creek. The day's chores were done, and it would be time for supper soon.

Suddenly, off in the distance, we heard the strains of what sounded like and old-time church organ, the kind that required the organist to pump the pedals with their feet to produce sound.

We immediately found this to be odd, because the nearest church was several miles away as the crow flies, and it would have been unusual for sound to travel such a great distance even in the quiet of the country.

Much to our amazement, the sound continued to grow louder and seemed to be moving up the holler we were in, heading toward us. Eventually, the sound was close enough that we could indeed tell it was an organ and was playing a song, although neither of us recognized the tune. The sound became louder and louder and eventually seemed to pass right over the top of us, apparently coming from an invisible source just above the treetops.

The musical notes continued playing as the still unseen object continued up the creek and then turned and went up across the ridge. The sound eventually faded into the distance until we could no longer hear it.

There were no roads nearby, and the sky was clear and cloudless, yet we both distinctly heard the song as the organ approached, flew directly over us (again, I'm guessing it was just above treetop level) and faded into the distance. There was nothing to see; it was only sound.

Needless to say, we were spooked by the entire incident and beat a hasty path back to the house, arriving just before supper. Leonard and I never told our parents, and only talked about it occasionally between ourselves. It was quite some time before we were brave enough to venture back to the area of the creek where we had been, but we never heard the invisible flying organ again.

To this day, I am at a loss for a logical explanation as to what we heard. I guess we'll never know what it was, but it sure frightened two young farm boys.

CHAPTER 2

THE CRYING KITTENS

When I was a child, we had an old cat that hung around in the barn on our property. One spring, she had a litter of kittens up in the hayloft, seven kittens in all. The old cat wasn't a very good mother and had abandoned the kittens, and unfortunately, they were already dead by the time my brother and sister and I found them. We felt sorry for the kittens and decided to have a funeral for them down by the creek bank.

We purloined one of mother's old hatboxes from the attic, filled it with straw, and placed all the tiny lifeless bodies inside. After arriving at the creek with our makeshift 'coffin,' we said a few words, and my older brother dug a hole with a shovel in the soft ground.

Sometime later, perhaps a week or more, my sister had gone to place some fresh-picked wildflowers on the tiny grave.

Imagine her surprise when she heard the sound of kittens meowing!

Thinking we had made a mistake and had buried the poor

kittens alive, she ran back to the house and got my brother and me. My brother grabbed the shovel out of the barn, and we flew down to the creek bank as fast as our feet would carry us. When we arrived, we could hear the faint sound of kittens, too.

My brother soon uncovered the box, and we quickly pulled it out of the ground and ripped the lid off the hatbox. Much to our shock, we were greeted with the sight—and smell—of seven very much deceased kittens. My sister took a stick and, holding her nose with one hand, gently prodded each tiny kitten. It was obvious they were all very dead.

Mystified, we replaced the box into the grave and covered it back up. From then on, for many years, we all continued to hear the muffled sounds of tiny kittens near the grave. We could only assume that what we were hearing was the ghosts of these poor tiny creatures.

CHAPTER 3

THE GIANT SNAKE

This happened when I was a much younger man, I'd say fifty or more years ago.

It was in the early spring, and I was out squirrel hunting in the woods with my .22 rifle.

I hadn't gotten many squirrels that day and observed that there wasn't hardly anything stirring in the woods, not even birds. I thought that maybe something had all the woodland creatures spooked, maybe a bobcat, as they were common in that part of the country at that time.

I shouldered my rifle and decided to make my way back to the house, figuring I'd just have to be content with the two or three squirrels I had bagged earlier.

At one point, I arrived at the creek and started following it back toward the house, figuring I still had a mile or more to go until I reached a place where it was shallow enough to ford.

I came upon a small clearing when I spied what I thought was a log lying across the creek. Surprised at this good fortune, I knew if I could cross the creek here, it would save me a lot of walking.

I was just about to step on the log to see if it would hold my weight—when the log moved! What I thought was a log turned out to be the biggest snake I've ever seen!

Stunned, I watched as the snake's tail came into view as it slithered across the creek. Now, this was in East Tennessee—we don't have snakes as big as telephone poles!

I wish I could have gotten a look at the snake's head, but by the time I came to my senses, I realized I had better get out of there—no wonder the creatures of the forest were spooked—as big as the snake looked, I was afraid it would try to eat me!

I made it back home and was met with disbelief when I told my tale of the giant snake, but I know what I saw. Years later, I saw a giant snake at a traveling carnival that was almost as big as the one I saw. It was, I believe, some from South America. The only thing I can figure out to explain my sighting was that the snake had escaped from another carnival. I never saw the giant snake again, but I was always extremely careful out in the woods after that.

CHAPTER 4

DISINTEGRATING PEOPLE

This is the story of the weirdest thing I've ever encountered in the woods. It was the summer after my freshman year of high school, and my friends and I often went to —— Park on —— ·Lake [exact location redacted at the original author's request] when the weather was nice.

The lakeside park backs up to another state park that has lots of hilly terrain covered with hiking trails. It had become kind of cloudy on this particular day, so my friend Jenny and I thought we might explore in the woods and maybe try some of the hiking trails.

As we ventured into the woods, we veered off the trail and came across what I can only describe as a primitive campsite. There was a lean-to made from pine boughs, a stone firepit, and evidence that someone had been there recently, namely empty Coke cans and snack food wrappers.

Jenny and I poked around the campsite for a bit and, growing bored, decided to venture farther toward the lake.

About a hundred yards from the campsite, we happened upon one of the scariest things I have ever seen in my life—there on the ground in the woods were two complete sets of human clothing, one male and one female, laid out as if the people were still in them.

The man's outfit consisted of a lightweight tan windbreaker, a button-up shirt with a yellow checked pattern, a white T-shirt, khaki pants, socks and brown leather shoes. The T-shirt was inside the checked shirt, which was tucked into the pants. There was even a belt in the pants. The socks were still in the bottom of the pant legs and went down into the shoes.

The woman's ensemble was just as creepy—a pale blue windbreaker over a printed dress, with tan-colored hose ending inside a pair of penny loafers.

Furthermore, the right arm of the man's clothing overlapped the left arm of the woman's clothing, giving the appearance that the couple had lain down on the forest floor and had been holding hands.

Now, there were no bones or anything like that, and the clothing still appeared to be in a fairly new state—it hadn't been in the woods very long.

We prodded the clothes with a stick and heard what sounded like loose change or maybe car keys jingle in the pocket of the man's khakis.

Suddenly overcome by fear, Jenny began crying and said we needed to leave, right now. I agreed. I was feeling totally scared and freaked out. It looked as if the couple had lain down and simply disappeared, leaving their clothing behind. By now, both of us were in tears, and we ran the rest of the way out of the woods.

We debated over several days as to what we should do—maybe call the cops? Or take some other friends back and show them what we had found? We scoured the local papers for weeks, but never turned up any information about a missing couple. In the end, we decided the best thing to do was to keep it to ourselves and never go back into the woods—and we never have and probably never will, although it has now been close to fifteen years since the incident occurred.

CHAPTER 5

THE SPIRIT TREE

I had gone on a trip to the Sequoyah Museum in Vonore, Tennessee, to do some research for a film script I'd been hired to write.

After I finished my research in the museum, I decided to stroll around the grounds for a bit and see what there was to see outside.

At one edge of the paved parking lot, there is an 'Indian Mound' where the remains of many Native Americans are interred. It's commemorated with a plaque, and there were many Native American objects left on the mound as tribute, items made from such things as bird feathers and deer sinew. I stood near the mound and contemplated these indigenous peoples and their fate.

Afterward, I decided to venture back into the woods behind the mound, seemingly drawn to a particular area for some unknown reason. After a short walk, I found myself in a clearing with the strangest tree I have ever encountered.

It was very large and very old, several feet around at the trunk. I'm unsure just what type of tree it was, but I think it may have been a beech tree. The tree was so massive and so otherworldly looking, it seemed totally out of place among the pine, oak and elm. The area beneath the tree was devoid of any plant life, covered instead by a thin layer of leaves over dark, fertile ground so barren otherwise that it gave the appearance of having been swept clean.

I knew right away that this was someone's 'power spot,' as I could feel the energy. This tree was so huge and so old and so magnificent that it seemed more like a Disney creation than an actual tree.

I stood at the base and meditated for a few moments, feeling the waves of energy, when I abruptly felt a darker, heavier presence, as if I was being watched. I suddenly was overcome with a mixture of fear and sadness. I felt like I was an intruder, and this was a sacred place, even though I am one-eighth Native American by birth on my father's side. I took a few pictures of the tree and then hurriedly left the area. Once I got home and looked at the digital pictures on my computer, I wasn't surprised to see what some call 'orbs' or spirit lights in the photos. I've visited the tree on a couple more occasions since, but always end up feeling like I'm somewhere I don't belong and beat a hasty retreat after a few minutes.

The tree, which has stood for hundreds of years—and I suspect will be there for hundreds more years to come—still stands and can be visited by anyone.

But if you do visit, please be reverent and respectful—there are protective spirits in these woods, and especially around this particular tree. If you visit it, you will immediately know what I'm speaking about to be true.

CHAPTER 6

NATIVE AMERICAN SPIRITS

It was Thanksgiving weekend, and my parents and I had traveled to the family farm to spend the holiday with my grandparents and some of my aunts and uncles and their children.

The farm was expansive and covered over 900 acres. In addition to many creeks and a river, there were also many natural features such as caves and bluffs, where centuries ago the Native Americans had hunted and lived.

My mom and dad and I were the first to arrive, and I decided to go out exploring while waiting for my older cousins, Jerry and James, to show up.

I considered walking down to cross the creek and mess around in one of the many livestock barns, but it had begun to spit snow, so I decided to go in the other direction down past the corncrib instead and visit one of the Indian bluffs that dotted the property. I made my way through the woods and down the steep bank above the bluff, carefully taking my time, as the snow was starting to stick a bit, which made for tricky going. I finally arrived and went under the bluff and decided to build a small fire in the ancient firepit to keep myself warm.

I ventured a little ways out into the woods, gathering dry twigs and pine cones with which to build my little fire. On my way back into the cavern-like area under the bluff, I thought I heard voices in the distance. I assumed Jerry and James had arrived and would soon be joining me.

I continued building my fire as planned, and soon had a nice little blaze going in the firepit, where the Native American inhabitants of centuries ago had cooked their meals. Every so often, I could still hear the sound of muffled voices in the distance.

Thinking nothing of it, I continued tending my small fire and looking around in the loose soil underneath the bluff, hoping to find a lost arrowhead or two—at the time it wasn't uncommon to find these much-prized pieces of worked flint.

I kicked at something in the dirt, thinking it might be an arrowhead, but it turned out to be a bone. Just as I pulled the bone from the dirt, the voices became louder. I walked to the opening of the bluff, expecting to see my cousins and share my find with them.

Looking this way and that, I could still hear the voices, but no one was in sight. At this point, the sounds seemed to be coming from the top of the bluff. I decided to walk back up and see if my cousins were on the top, perhaps trying to find the way I had used to climb down.

When I reached the top of the bluff, however, there was still no sign of my cousins. I could still hear the muffled voices, but now they seemed to be coming from the bottom of the bluff instead of the top. At first I was a little perplexed, but thought maybe Jerry and James had gone down the other side, and we had missed each other in the process. So I began the task of making my way back down, taking my time, as there was a good dusting of snow on the path now, which made for slippery going —one wrong move and I could slide all the way down the steep hill past the bluff, ending up getting soaked in the creek and maybe even injuring myself in the bargain.

Picking my way along carefully, I made it back to the entrance to the cave and found myself still alone. What was going on? I immediately thought of the bone that I had found, which I had stuck into my jacket pocket. It suddenly occurred to me that this might be human remains. It wasn't impossible, but to my knowledge only one skeleton had been found in the cave years ago. The skeleton had been buried sitting up, suggesting the body had been that of a Native American chief.

Under the bluff, I could still hear the muffled conversation, and as I strained to listen, it began to sound more and more like English was not the language being spoken. This sent shivers up my spine.

Hurriedly, I replaced the bone in the soft earth where I had found it, and covered it well. In my mind I apologized to whomever or whatever I had disturbed. I had the growing feeling that I needed to leave this place as soon as possible, which I did, as soon as I'd put out my little fire.

When I got back to my grandparents' house, my cousins had just arrived and were still helping their parents carry food out of the car and into the house. I spent the rest of the evening pondering the events of the day, and the next morning when my cousins wanted to go exploring, I refused to go anywhere near the bluff. I never told them the reason, but they didn't seem to mind, as there were lots of other places to explore.

I was a grown man before I ever ventured back under the bluff again, although during those later occasions I did not hear any more voices—and I also took care not to disturb any areas that I thought may be sacred to my ancestors.

CHAPTER 7

THE ABANDONED HOUSE

This happened in the mountains of North Carolina. My husband at the time was in the military, and we were stationed at Camp Lejeune. One weekend, we and another military couple decided to go camping in the rugged Appalachian Mountains on the other side of the state. After setting up camp, we decided to hike around for a bit in the hilly, mountainous terrain.

Deep in the woods in a little hollow, imagine our surprise when we chanced upon an abandoned Victorian house. It was almost overgrown with kudzu vines, but we still managed to find a way inside and decided to explore.

Once in, we were amazed at the surprisingly good condition of the inside of the house. Upon further inspection, we found the house to be fully furnished, and also found clothing and even old children's toys. It was more than a little creepy, and we all got the feeling we shouldn't be there—it was if the people who lived there had just stepped out and would return at any moment.

Our husbands were just as mystified as we girls were, although they didn't seem as scared. My husband, Richard, even began checking the walls for any hidden passages, thinking perhaps the family had gone into hiding for some reason and then perished, trapped inside the walls.

I can't express how much the house still looked lived-in. There was clothing laid out on the still-made beds, and plates and silverware set out on the dinner table. Everything was covered with a somewhat heavy layer of dust, however, so it was obvious the place hadn't been lived in for decades. This was in the early 1960s, although the musty calendar on the kitchen wall was from 1909. Was it even possible that no one had enter this dwelling in over fifty years?

The longer we spent in the house, the more scared my female friend and I became, eventually becoming almost hysterical. Eventually, after much pleading, our husbands decided we should leave, although they would have been happier to stay and explore the house more.

After we had left and the shivers wore off, all we could discuss on the drive back home was how isolated the house was —it was literally in the middle of the woods, and the nearest paved highway was miles away.

A few weeks later, our husbands planned a trip back—alone —to continue exploring. My friend and I were fine with that.

Although I was curious about the house, I had no desire to visit again after the sense of fright that had enveloped me there.

However, when the guys came back home the Sunday evening after their planned trip, the story became even stranger. Although they were sure of the exact location, they had been unable to find the house and had spent the entire weekend wandering the woods.

Even though they remembered and recognized natural land-marks, no trace of the house could be found.

They even stopped at a roadside general store a dozen or so miles from where the house had been, and when they inquired about the house, the proprietor emphatically denied that any such house existed. When my husband and his friend persisted, the man at the general store suddenly became angry and told them to leave, adding that if they knew what was good for them, they should forget the house and never come back!

They ignored the warning and went back on two other occasions, but could never find the house again. And, like the owner of the general store, any of the locals whom they chanced upon and asked about the place refused to talk about or even acknowledge it.

I know what we saw, and I know that it was real. But not being able to find it again and the local folks not wanting to talk about it only adds to the mystery—did we chance upon the site of some unspeakable tragedy? I may never know the answer, but I will always wonder about the abandoned house deep in the woods.

CHAPTER 8

FOOTPRINTS IN THE SNOW

The weirdest thing that I ever saw in the woods happened when I was just a boy, maybe ten or eleven years old.

It had snowed heavily the night before, so I was enjoying a day off from school (it had been canceled due to the weather) by walking around in the early morning snow-covered silence.

I was quite a ways back in the woods, maybe a mile or so, when I happened upon some footprints.

They were human footprints, but smaller than my feet, so I assumed they belonged to a child of maybe five or six years old. And to top it off, whoever had left the prints in the snow had been barefoot! It was about 34 degrees and much too cold for anyone—let alone a child—to be out wandering barefoot, in the snow, no less.

I noticed right away that there were no footprints—bare or otherwise—leading up to where the tiny footprints began. I followed the prints for a few hundred yards—where they abruptly ended in a small clearing. I looked all around, even up in the trees, but could find no trace of the small child who had made the prints. I followed them back again to where they began, still just as mystified as ever.

Still puzzled, I made my way over to my friend's house and told him about what I had seen. He got dressed for the weather, and we both trekked back out into the woods.

When we arrived, the footprints were still visible, but just barely. The freshly falling snow was filling them in. We scoured the entire area for maybe a square mile, but never found more footprints or any evidence of the child who had made the ones we both observed. To this day, I still can find no rational explanation. That's my story of the weirdest thing I ever encountered in the woods, and I'm glad I have a witness who will back it up!

CHAPTER 9

EVIL IN THE WOODS

The weirdest, creepiest stuff I ever found in the woods happened when I was a teenager. I'd only been driving a few years and had an old '71 Chevrolet Impala. It was a road boat and gas guzzler for sure, but I loved to get out at night and drive around by the moonlight.

There was an abandoned subdivision tract I had found during my ramblings, and I decided to go back one night and check it out. There were no houses, only what seemed like miles of paved road that went far back into the hills. The original developer had gone bankrupt, which was why it was left in the state it was in, all the building lots long since overgrown with brush and sapling pines.

On this particular night, I had found the furthest extreme of the paved road blocked by a fallen tree. Feeling somewhat adventurous, I got out of my car with a flashlight to see if the tree could be moved. However, it was a beast of an old rotten oak and must have weighed close to a ton. There was no way I could move it by myself. Deciding that I wasn't finished exploring for the night, I decided to lock my car and go ahead on foot. I figured since the road was blocked, I was safe, as there would be no one else in the area.

After about half a mile, the pavement stopped and continued on as a gravel road leading up a steep hill.

I sallied forth, undaunted, happily stomping along in the gravel while enjoying the noise it made as it crunched beneath my boots.

At the top of the hill, the gravel road ended as well, and now the road became nothing more than a rutted path through the high weeds and briars, with huge trees flanking either side. I was still feeling adventurous and decided to press on, determined to see how far I could go and where I would eventually end up.

About a half mile along the footpath, it curved sharply to the right. At the corner where it curved, I was playing my flashlight over the woods when the beam suddenly struck something out of the ordinary. On the slope of a short, steep bank, someone had fashioned a crude arrow shape out of some logs and branches of varying size. It looked too perfect to be random, so I was sure it was some kind of trail marker. I debated for a couple of minutes, then decided to abandon the path and see where the primitive 'trail maker' led.

At the crest of the bank where the arrow pointed, I found another narrow but well-worn path, which led deeper into the woods. I forged ahead, enjoying the adventure and solace that comes with being out in nature. The path twisted and turned a bit, but was leading uphill, to the top of a ridge.

When I arrived at the top after a good half hour of hiking, I thought I would perhaps be met with a vista overlooking the city or the nearby lake. Instead, what I found made my blood run cold.

Where the ground leveled out, in a fairly large clearing, was a gigantic pentagram made from carefully arranged logs—I mean this thing was huge! There were other logs set up outside the circle of the pentagram, which reminded me of altars. There were also upside-down crosses planted at various spots.

By now, I was actually sweating and shaking, jumping at every sound I heard and playing my flashlight all over the trees, trying to catch sight of anyone who might be hiding.

I caught a glimpse of something in the middle of the large pentagram and shined my light on it for a better look—it turned out to be the remains of some large bird, perhaps even a duck or a goose, which had been burned. I realized that whoever had done all this was serious about it—it was too intricate for just some metalhead kids messing about out in the woods. This was some sort of Satanic-type cult or group or whatever, which met to perform blood sacrifices.

I decided it was high time I got out of there, and I started moving as fast as I dared back through the woods.

After what seemed like hours, I finally arrived back at my car. Written in mud across my windshield was a single word: BEWARE. I grabbed an old T-shirt out of the back seat and scrubbed it off the best I could and then jumped in, silently praying my car would start. Thankfully it did, and I'm sure I broke the speed limit all the way home.

I've never shared my experience with anyone, and I never went exploring anywhere near the derelict subdivision or surrounding woods again. It still frightens me to this day to even think about what might have happened if I had shown up on the wrong night or at the wrong time and happened across these people and their evil practices in the woods.

I still have a sense of adventure, but learned some very valuable lessons that night—never go exploring alone, always let someone at home know where you're going, and realize that there are some things that are better left alone—people who do things in secret and hidden out of sight do so for a reason.

As the crudely written message on my car windshield stated —BEWARE!

CHAPTER 10

THE MONSTER IN THE WOODS

This was back in the late sixties, and my friend Eddie and I had taken our dogs out hunting at night. We were hunting coons and possum, and the dogs were well trained at treeing those animals.

It was about two o'clock in the morning and we hadn't had much luck. We had walked all the way across the farmlands and ended up at the edge of the river.

We decided to take a break on the riverbank and let the dogs run free for a bit, to see if they could flush any animals out of hiding.

We sat on a high bank overlooking the river, smoked a couple of cigarettes, and just listened to the sounds of the rushing water below. After about an hour, we started getting tired and decided we had better call the dogs and then start making our way back home.

This was where it started getting weird.

First of all, when we called the dogs, they wouldn't come. Anyone who's ever used hounds to hunt coon or possum knows that these dogs will come when called even if they have an animal treed. Our dogs, four in all, would come to within maybe a couple dozen yards of where we were standing on the river-bank, but wouldn't come any closer. We started walking down to where the dogs were, and when we came upon them, we saw that they were frightened and whimpering and even had their tails between their legs. Now these dogs weren't exactly fero-cious, like a pit bull or anything, but coonhounds tend to be very brave—I've had several dogs who have lost chunks of their ears and have also been bitten and clawed on their muzzles and snouts. Both coons and possum will put up a fight to the finish, even against a creature that is several times their size.

But these dogs were scared, I mean truly scared, and it was definitely something we were not used to seeing out of other-wise great and valuable hunting dogs. About this time, we heard a commotion on the bank by where we had just been sitting. It sounded like a large animal was coming up the bank.

The dogs grew even more afraid and were now cowering behind our legs and letting out high-pitched yelps and whines.

The batteries on Eddie's flashlight had already given out, but mine was still working, although somewhat dimly. I flashed the beam over the area to see what was making the noise.

In the dim beam, I saw what looked like a man (or at least the shape of one), but unlike any man I had ever seen. He would have had to be between eight and ten feet tall. I called out, asking the person to identify himself, and also stated that we were armed. The thing just stood there, as if it was eying us.

The dogs, although now on leashes, were still making a racket and trying to pull us away. After there was no response, I fired a shot into the air.

Whatever it was didn't budge, but instead let out a low, groaning noise, almost a growl. Whatever it was, it sounded hostile.

We tried to set the dogs on it, but that was a lost cause—the hounds were out of their minds with fear at this point, even wetting themselves. Suddenly, I noticed a stench. It was way worse than any skunk I had ever smelled, more like rotting garbage. Eddie and I fired two more shots, one each, in the general direction of the creature.

At this point it let out a loud yowl, which made the hair stand up on my arms.

I let the dogs go, and they took off back towards where our pickup truck was parked. The beast suddenly turned and jumped or dove off the bank, and we heard a huge splash as it hit the water.

Shaken, Eddie and I decided now would be a good time to make ourselves scarce, and we headed back for the truck. We got the dogs rounded up and got out of there.

I've told the story to several people, some of whom concluded we ran into a bear. This doesn't sound right to me—first of all, there are no bears in this area, and certainly not any that would be that large. Furthermore, what little of it I was able to catch sight of in the light of the flashlight, it looked like a man, only very big and very tall. There have been no further sightings I'm aware of in the area, but due to the size of the creature, the unique smell and the noises it made, I think we came across a Bigfoot. I've read similar stories about how dogs react to the creature as well, and that further convinced me. It wasn't scared of us, our dogs, or our guns—so I certainly don't want to encounter it again under those circumstances.

CHAPTER 11

THE LAKE MONSTER

One day my friend Scotty and I were out messing around in the woods with our BB guns. We had hiked out into the woods over by the lake. It was starting to get dark, so it would soon be time to go home, as we didn't want to be wandering around in the woods after dark.

We found that the quickest way home would be to walk around the shore of the lake rather than cutting back through the woods—it was probably a little bit farther in distance, but the walking would all be on level ground instead of climbing the hills and ridges on the trek through the woods, thus saving us some time.

We had just rounded a point of land and headed into a small cove that we thought would lead us back to the paved road. The sun was starting to set, but we weren't as worried about it getting dark, since we were familiar with the area we were now in.

Just as we came up the side of the cove, we heard a splashing in the water. It wasn't unusual for fish to jump up out of the lake sometimes, so at first we didn't think too much about it. However, the splashing continued, and when we got around the bend where we could see, we were met with an unusual sight.

Out in the water, in about the middle of the cove, something was moving up and down in the water, making a greater and greater commotion. At first I thought it might be a turtle, as snappers weren't uncommon in the area, and some can grow to a pretty large size. As we continued watching, it became evident that this wasn't a turtle, at least not like any we had ever seen.

We observed the beast's back or 'hump' moving briskly up and down in the water, making a fairly large wake around whatever it was. From the part that we could see, however, it would have had to have been the size of a small car, maybe a Volkswagen Beetle!

We stood and stared at it for a good fifteen minutes, too dumbstruck to do much else. Eventually, the hump submerged with a large splash and left a sizable wake on top of the water as it swam away.

We hightailed it out of there and made it back to the paved road in record time. We went back on several occasions throughout the rest of the year, now always carrying binoculars and a Polaroid camera.

Unfortunately, we never spotted whatever it was again. Short of a giant sea turtle (which was very unlikely, since we were hundreds of miles inland from the coast), I don't know of anything else to which our 'monster' could be compared.

CHAPTER 12

STRANGENESS IN THE SMOKIES

I've spent a great deal of time hiking in the Great Smoky Mountains National Park, on both the Eastern Tennessee and Western North Carolina sides. The mountains derive their name from the 'smoke' that seems to hang in the trees of the deep forest. From what I've heard, the Cherokee gave the mountains this name.

Now, the Smokies are a vast expanse of wilderness. It's easy to get lost and turned around there—I can attest to this fact, having been temporarily lost a few times myself.

There are also some unexplained disappearances in the mountains—a brief search online will give you more info, bringing up such tragic missing person stories as young Dennis Martin, teenager Treeny Gibson, and retiree Thelma Melton. These people have been missing for decades, and no trace of them was ever found.

I mention that to tell you this—there is a strangeness to the mountains.

There are places that, although they represent nature at its finest, also have a very eerie, creepy feeling. I've experienced it firsthand on many occasions.

One memorable instance that springs to mind was when I made one of my many hikes up to Clingman's Dome, the highest point in the park. It's a tough hike, the trail feeling like you're almost walking straight up in places. The incline is so steep in some parts, you can literally reach out and touch the trail in front of you as you ascend.

On one particular occasion, I had inexplicably decided to wander a little ways off the trail, having seen some beautiful mountain laurel plants in a nearby hollow. Now, like I was saying, it's very easy to become disoriented in the deep woods, and going off the trail is not recommended for even the most seasoned mountain hiker. But, even knowing better, off I went, thinking I'd just walk in a straight line and therefore make it easy to find my way back to the trail.

I made it to the hollow and was admiring the mountain laurel patch when I decided to venture up the bank and see what was above the little hollow. As I cleared the top of the bank, I spotted an ancient oak tree off in the distance. I decided to go have a look at the massive giant of a tree, which was easily centuries old.

As I stood looking up at the towering oak, I noticed a little path leading off to one side, probably left by deer or other animals that live in the park. I ducked under the overhang in the brush and pushed my way along the little game trail.

The trail ended and I found myself in a small clearing, and this is where it gets weird—it was suddenly as if the whole forest became silent. I didn't hear a bird or the wind in the leaves or anything—it was the most deafening silence I have ever encountered.

I stood in the clearing a long time, marveling at the silence—

it was like being in a vacuum. Suddenly I felt very drowsy and had to fight off the urge to just stretch out and go to sleep. It was as if the woods were lulling me into a dreamlike state.

Eventually, the strange paralysis seemed to lift, and I began to hear the noises of the forest again. I made my way back to the trail, somewhat alarmed that the sun was starting to set—all in all, I figured I must have stood transfixed for over an hour, at least. I often wonder if I might have a period of 'missing time' regarding this episode.

So if you find yourself in the Great Smoky Mountains National Park, take care and notice your surroundings and be wary of the mystical effects of the park. I feel like if I had followed temptation and stretched out for a nap, I might have been one of those souls who are lost and never heard from again.

CHAPTER 13

THE HAUNTED CABIN

I'll tell you about something that happened to me one time that was really weird, really strange. It was fall of the year, I know, because I was out in the woods hunting ginseng, and that's the time of year to look for it—the berries have turned red and it's easy to spot. A friend of mine had a big piece of property, several hundred acres, that was nothing but woods. He used to lease it out to deer hunters during hunting season. He gave me permission to hunt for ginseng on this property.

I was way back in the woods, following a dry creek bed. In spring, during the rainy season, the creek was pretty good sized, but this time of year it was dry, so the going was fairly easy, although it was a little bit rocky.

Once far enough back into the woods, I started side trips up the bank to look for ginseng plants in the shade of trees and rocks where it was likely to grow. I had dug several good-sized roots and was spurred on by dollar signs in my head for every root I dug. Ginseng is highly sought after, and the dried roots are worth almost their weight in gold.

On one of my side trips, I came across the remains of a one-room cabin, what most people would call a shack. This was in the heart of Appalachia, and at one time all the hills and hollers around here were dotted with tiny structures like this, where poor families lived without any electricity or running water.

This particular cabin had no doors or windows remaining, just holes where they once had been. Most of the roof was still intact, and the walls and floor were still in passable shape. I stepped in and had a look around, just to see what I could see. As it turned out, there was absolutely nothing inside, not a stick of furniture or belongings or anything to suggest people had ever lived here.

I stepped back out and started on my way up the hill, when I heard what sounded like heavy footsteps on the wooden floor of the cabin. I stopped and turned around and went back, figuring someone else (perhaps another ginseng hunter) was trying to play a trick on me. I snuck up beside the cabin and poked my head into one of the open window holes. The cabin was still just as empty as when I had been in it just a couple of minutes before. I walked all the way around the structure, but there was no one there. I just kind of shrugged it off and started walking again.

When I was just a few yards away, I heard it again, the sounds of someone walking across the cabin floor. This time it was accompanied by a noise that sounded like someone dragging a wooden chair across the floor too, a familiar kind of noise if you've ever lived in a house with wooden floors (which I had).

Again, I snuck back to the cabin, but this time I quickly ran around to the front door. This was the only door, so if someone was inside, this was the only way out. Again, the cabin was just as bare and empty as before. I had heard the noises continue right up to just before I stepped inside.

The third time I started to walk away, I heard both noises again, and I also heard what sounded like a small child whisper, "Daddy?" It was more of a question than a statement, I could tell just by the way it was said.

Again, I went back. I thought maybe some kid was hiding or was perhaps even trapped. I didn't have any kids at the time, so I knew if someone was expecting 'daddy,' then they weren't talking to me anyway. And again, the cabin was totally empty, and the noises stopped when I stepped in. I even checked the floorboards, and none of them were loose. Outside, the cabin was high enough off the ground that I could see all the way under it. There was just no place a person, even a child, could hide.

I turned and left again, and the noises started back up. This time, however, I just kept walking, and I heard the noises until I was out of earshot.

I've had people ask me if I was afraid, but the answer is no, I wasn't. I'm not scared of any haint, spook, booger or ghost. I've been all through these woods, and the only thing I might be afraid of is a snake, and I'm not even afraid of them if I can find a stick. Later, I told my friend who owned the property about what happened, and he said he'd heard about similar encounters.

He also added that the story he had heard was that the people who once lived there all died suddenly, the whole family wiped out by smallpox or cholera or something, but that it had been decades ago. He said he was not only afraid to go in there, but wouldn't even go near the woods where the cabin was located—he said he'd rather walk a mile out of his way than pass by it. I just laughed at him and told him ghosts can't hurt the living, but they can make you hurt yourself if you try to run off scared!

CHAPTER 14

THE CRYING BABY

Back when I was a young man, people around where we lived in the mountain community of Ramsey talked about an abandoned, haunted house way out in the middle of the woods. The story was that a woman had gone crazy and killed her baby one night during a storm and had buried the infant in the cellar.

The legend also stated that if you visited the house on a stormy night, you could still hear a baby crying.

My friends and I got our courage up, and the next time it stormed, we went off to find the house and see if we could hear the baby crying. It was pouring rain like mad when we struck out through the woods, lightning dancing all around and thunder booming to beat the band. It was a pretty good hike back into the mountains where the remains of the old house were located, maybe two or three miles, but we plunged ahead in stony silence, dripping wet but determined to experience the legend for ourselves. We were just a bunch of young bucks out to prove our bravery and that we weren't afraid of anything.

We reached the old abandoned house shortly before midnight, and the storm was still going full force. The house did look pretty scary; with all the windows knocked out, it looked like a giant mouth missing a few teeth. We piled inside; at least we were in out of the pounding rain and howling storm. It would have been scary, I imagine, even if we didn't know the legend about the woman and her baby.

Sure enough, right after a big crack of lightning hit nearby, we heard a sound that sounded exactly like a baby crying. All the hair stood up on my neck, and I'll never forget how lonesome and pitiful the crying sounded. There were seven of us boys altogether, but when that baby started crying, it was easy to see who the cowards were—four of the fellows ran off into the night as fast as their legs would carry them. Myself and two other guys stayed behind.

I'll admit I was scared, and I know the others who stayed were scared too, but we were determined to see if we could locate the source of the crying. I kept telling myself that maybe it was a cat or some type of bird, and maybe we just thought it sounded like a baby because that's what we wanted to believe.

We looked over the entire house, top to bottom, but were unable to find the source of the crying baby.

When we finally gave up and left, we were just as mystified as before, perhaps even more so. We never were able to go back and look again—about a month or two after our little expedition, the house was struck by lightning and burned to the ground.

After that, I never heard any more reports of the crying baby —but I know for a fact that there was something strange there, for I heard it with my own ears.

CHAPTER 15

THE LIGHT IN THE COFFIN

A long time ago, I was seeing this young lady who lived several miles away, and I had stayed at her house a little later than I had planned one Sunday evening after church. Back in my day, we called it 'courting' or 'sparking.'

Basically, it meant that we weren't old enough to actually date, so it was how couples got to know each other under the watchful eye of parents. I guess things sure have changed since then.

Anyway, it was late, probably about eleven at night, and I had a long walk ahead of me via the old country roads. Knowing I had to be up early Monday morning to do my farm chores, I was already regretting staying so late, so I had the bright idea to cut through the woods and try to save myself some time.

I wasn't scared of the woods, I had played in them since I was just a little boy, and as I got older, I also often hunted in these same woods and fished on the bordering lake. So off I went through the woods, hoping I'd get home in time to at least get four or five hours' sleep before I had to get up and milk the cows. Life on the farm starts early!

I was coming up through a small hollow when I noticed something odd off to my right. I was following a little trail, and whatever I was seeing was farther off into the woods. As I got closer, I saw what appeared to me to be a coffin, with a glowing light inside!

Well, needless to say, it shook me up pretty badly. I was so scared that I just started running. I ran through saw briars, tripped over rocks and roots, you name it, and I either plowed through it or fell over it. By the time I got home, I sure was a mess—scratched, cuts all over, bleeding and so on. I had even torn the knees out of my good Sunday pants. I was still so scared of what I had witnessed that I was sweating and shaking all over.

I almost hate to admit it now, but back then, most of my family were superstitious. Not so much my dad, but my mother was extremely superstitious, and I guess it rubbed off on me. I was sure that I had witnessed some strange omen that foretold my death. Still, I was scared silly, and with tears on my cheeks, I hesitantly awakened my parents and told them what I had seen.

As expected, my superstitious mother started panicking and crying, thinking that I (or someone else in the family) was a goner for sure. My dad wasn't happy at being woken up, but he dragged himself out of bed and started getting dressed. Like I said, he wasn't very superstitious and wanted to put an end to this before the whole house was in an uproar.

I didn't want to go back out and was already sure I wouldn't last through the night. But my dad prevailed, and soon we were back out in the woods, retracing my route. Before long, we reached the area, and I saw the slowly blinking light. My heart began to race—I knew it was for real now.

My dad left me on the path and ventured closer. Suddenly,

he let out a loud laugh. That kind of shocked me even more—how could he find this funny? Still chuckling, he called me over, assuring me everything was going to be okay.

Reluctantly, I joined him.

"There's your coffin with a light in it," he said, putting a hand on my shoulder. I looked over and saw what he was talking about—on the ground was a half-rotted log, with a firefly caught in a spiderweb inside it. Boy, did I ever feel foolish!

To this day, I'm no longer superstitious, despite being raised that way by my mother. My father has passed on now, but I will forever be in his debt for going back out into the woods with me that night. If he hadn't discovered it was just a lightning bug caught in a spiderweb in a half-rotted, hollow log, I probably would have died of fright.

CHAPTER 16

THE PETRIFIED PIG

When I was just a little girl, we had an old sow that took sick then wandered off into the woods and died. It wasn't like she was a pet or anything, so I soon forgot about her and thought nothing more of it.

Years later, one of our chickens had escaped from the pen and was happily making her home in the woods surrounding our house. I'd catch sight of her now and again, but anytime I tried to catch her, she would run off into the brush and escape.

I figured that since she was a laying hen, she had probably nested somewhere in the woods and left her eggs out there somewhere. There wasn't a lot to do back in those days—we had to make our own fun—so finding fresh eggs in the woods had kind of become a game for me.

Well, on this particular day of playing 'find-the-eggs,' I had ventured farther into the woods than usual. I could hear the hen clucking, and followed the sound, winding this way and that. I stepped through a row of midsized cedar trees into a small clearing—and there was the old sow!

I couldn't believe my eyes. She had gone missing at least two years before, but here she was on the ground in front of me—whole. She looked as if she had just lain down and gone to sleep, and other than being smashed flat on the side she was lying on and the gray pallor of her skin, she looked just like she always did.

I couldn't believe she hadn't rotted away, and I looked around until I found a small branch off a tree to poke her with. Believe it or not, the old sow was as hard as a rock!

I'm not sure if she was mummified or petrified, but she was solid as could be, if not a little hollow sounding. I wasn't brave enough to touch her with my bare hands, but prodded around as much as I could with my stick.

I often went back and observed the pig on several instances through the years, and she always looked the same, no matter the season. One day, however, when I entered the little clearing, the pig was completely gone. There was nothing left but a dark spot on the ground that perfectly reproduced her outline. I have no idea what happened to her, but my best guess would be that someone else found her and made her part of a sideshow somewhere.

Probably made a pretty penny off of her, I'd imagine.

That's the strangest thing I've ever seen in the woods, and I'm almost ninety years old. I wouldn't have believed it if I hadn't witnessed it for myself.

CHAPTER 17

BIGFOOT IN FENTRESS COUNTY

One of my distant cousins inherited a large farm in Fentress County, Tennessee, from his mother's side of the family. He worked as a banker in nearby Knoxville, but liked to 'play farmer,' as I called it, on the weekends.

Through the week, he hired me to be the caretaker, and my job was to feed and water the livestock, which was comprised of several hundred head of cattle and a few workhorses.

One weekday evening, a fellow who lived on a nearby farm had cut his leg very badly after a mishap with a chainsaw. He called for an ambulance, and I heard it coming down the common gravel road that the farms shared.

He'd cut his leg fairly deeply, and the ambulance crew decided to transport him to the local hospital several miles away. When the ambulance had first arrived, they were running lights but no siren. On the way back out, however, they had the siren going as well.

I was standing on the front porch of the farmhouse and

watched the ambulance go by with the neighbor inside. The loud sound of the siren was quite a racket out here in the country, where normally everything is very quiet.

After the ambulance passed, I started to go back in the house, when I heard another sound off in the distance. It sort of sounded like the ambulance siren, but was coming from a direction way off into the woods.

Whatever it was, it put up quite a howl and made the hair on my neck stand up. It continued for a good fifteen minutes or so after the actual ambulance was out of earshot. I was glad when it finally hushed, and I didn't think much more about it after that.

Several weeks pass by, and one evening I was over at a nearby friend's house, watching television via satellite. He was flipping through the channels and just happened to stop on a Bigfoot documentary.

There was a Bigfoot researcher on the show who claimed to have recorded the sound of a Bigfoot creature howling in the wilderness. When he played the audio, I once again felt the hair stand up on my neck—it sounded exactly the same as the howl I'd heard after the ambulance had went by when the other farmer had sliced his leg!

Before I could say anything, my friend started talking excitedly—he said he'd heard the same kind of yowls in the woods around these parts. When I related my story about the ambulance, he knew exactly what I was talking about—we had both heard the same sound but on different occasions.

Now to my knowledge, there have been no Bigfoot sightings in Fentress County, but there are at least two people who have heard the exact same howl as what the researcher played on the documentary. These days, I always take a pistol with me when I'm out tending to the livestock—just in case.

CHAPTER 18

THE MYSTERIOUS BALL

Back when I was a boy, there wasn't any such thing as a school bus out in the country. If you went to school, you had to walk. Some kids had it better, some worse, but I lived about three miles from school, if I took the gravel road.

On this particular spring day, when school ended, instead of walking back via the gravel road, I decided to go through the woods. In my mind I considered it a shortcut, but in reality it was probably even farther, especially the route I took. I had a slingshot that I had carved myself, and I wanted to see if I could find anything to shoot at in the woods on the way home.

I was just ambling along, taking shots at birds, trees, whatever, but soon ran out of stones. With no ammo, I figured I might as well head on to the house.

As I walked through a small clearing, I heard something coming through the woods off to my right flank.

Since I was getting close to home, I thought it might be my brother. He was already finished with school and worked at a nearby sawmill, and he often walked home through the woods. I called out his name, but got no response, although the noise continued getting closer.

All of a sudden, something I can only describe as a giant ball, about five or six feet high, rolled up on top of some small pines and came to rest. I couldn't tell what it was made of, but it was perfectly round and seemed to be blue and white striped, like old-time overalls.

As I stood looking at it, it was as if it noticed me, and then it rolled slowly backwards out of sight, the pine trees snapping back into place and hiding it from view. Again, I thought my brother might be trying to scare me, so I called out his name. Again, no response, but I could still hear the ball or whatever it was rolling around in the bushes, although it stayed out of sight.

I was pretty scared at this point, so I took off running in the direction that I knew would lead me to the gravel road. I'd had enough adventure in the woods at this point. Once I'd reached the gravel road, I didn't stop running and ran all the way to the house.

When I got there, my brother was sitting at the kitchen table finishing dinner, so there was no way whatever I had seen could have been him.

I have no idea what it was, and I never saw it again. It appeared sentient, as it had rolled backwards after 'seeing' me. I don't guess I'll ever know what it was.

CHAPTER 19

THE PIPER IN THE PARK

Big Ridge State Park is located in eastern Tennessee, not too far from the Norris Dam area. I have been to the park on many occasions and have hiked all of the available trails and taken in the sights.

There are many legends about the park, including a ghostly dog, a phantom horse, and even human apparitions at the old grist mill. I've never experienced any of the hauntings, but I have heard what they call the Piper.

The Piper is usually heard in the park in the summertime, just after sundown.

It sounds like someone trilling tuneless notes on a flute or perhaps a penny whistle.

The sound is certainly eerie, and it will give you goose-bumps for sure. I've had people try to explain that it's just someone practicing their playing in the park, but the fact of the matter is that it has been heard for many decades.

If you want to hear it for yourself, go into the park some

summer evening and park in the lot down by the old gristmill. Roll your car windows almost all the way up (I don't know why, but you can hear the sound better if the windows are just slightly cracked instead of being all the way down) and just wait.

Many people have heard the Piper, but no one has ever solved the mystery of this seemingly paranormal happening.

CHAPTER 20

THE FLOATING COFFIN

This happened back when I was a little girl. My older sister, Dosha, and I were out picking blackberries in the woods. It was a pretty bushy area, and we had to be careful and watch for snakes, as there are poisonous copperheads in this part of the country.

We were up high on the edge of a steep bank overlooking the river, and just about had our baskets full, so it would be time to head home soon.

All of a sudden, Dosha shrieked and dropped her basket, spilling her berries all over the ground. I looked up to see what was the matter, figuring she had probably seen a snake, and I was hoping she hadn't been bitten.

Her eyes were big and she had both hands over her mouth. Before I could ask what was wrong, she pointed down below toward an old railroad bed. It took me a few seconds to see what she was pointing at, but then I saw it too. It was a coffin making its way along the roadbed, seemingly floating in the air.

You talk about scared! Dosha didn't even take the time to pick up her basket, much less her berries, and we ran through the woods, screaming as if the devil himself were after us.

We made it back home after what seemed like an eternity, and explained to our mother (as best we could between sobs) what we had seen. My mother seemed frightened too, but was eventually able to calm us down and convince us we must have seen something else.

But Dosha and I knew better—we knew what a coffin looked like. Back then they were made out of pine and painted black. I don't know if it was a warning or a sign, but a few days later an old woman who lived a few miles farther up the roadbed where we had seen the coffin died unexpectedly. We never went berry picking in that area again.

CHAPTER 21

ANGEL HAIR

I've got one for you. I've heard of as well as seen plenty of weird stuff out in the woods (including a grown man, naked except for tube socks and a clown mask, carefully making his way through a briar patch), but this story is the strangest by far that I have personally encountered.

I was out traipsing about in the woods one day with my dog, not hunting or anything, but just bored and looking for something to get into. My dog had run off ahead of me out of sight and was barking at something, so I went to have a look.

As I came into a small clearing, it looked like someone had dumped clear cotton candy all over several trees. The strands were not as fine as a spiderweb, nor as thick as fishing line, but somewhere in between.

The strands were sticky to the touch, and large clumps of them were falling from the trees, where they basically just melted into the earth.

I couldn't help but notice some of the strands extended into the sky above the tops of the trees, and went high enough into the sky to be out of sight. I tried to gather some of it in, but like I said, it basically just melted to the touch.

I've read about other people finding it online, but no one has any idea what it really is. Some scientists claim that it's strands of web left by migrating spiders that ride the air currents, but I never saw the first spider and I shiver to think just how many arachnids it would take to leave such huge clumps and strands of the material.

Other folks claim that it's something the military is doing, testing radar signals or something, but I have my doubts about that. Still another school of thought ties them into UFO activity, but I certainly didn't hear of any UFOs in the area at that time.

I'm sure there is some sort of logical, scientific explanation for it, but it's just something that hasn't been fully proven or discovered yet. Still, it was a really weird sight to see.

CHAPTER 22

PHANTOM HORSES

When I was in the sixth grade, my family and I moved into an old farmhouse on the edge of some deep woods in Arkansas. Not long after moving in, I began hearing strange noises outside at night when I was trying to go to sleep. It sounded like horses galloping by in the woods back behind the house.

I told my mother and father about it, but they just kind of laughed it off and attributed it to me getting the jitters from never having lived out in the country before. Still, I know what I heard, and I was sure it was the unmistakable sound of hoofbeats.

One day, while exploring in the woods, I found a small cave quite a ways out from where we lived. There were initials and dates from the 1800s scratched into the walls. I visited the cave on several different jaunts into the woods over the years, but always left after becoming frightened. I wasn't sure what about it scared me, other than being a kid with an overactive imagination in a cave deep in the woods.

We eventually moved away, going up north so my parents could find work, and I forgot all about the hoofbeats and the cave. Years later, all grown up, I was watching a documentary about ghosts and Civil War hauntings. And there, believe it or not, was the old farm we had lived on!

My eyes almost bugged out of my head. The man they were interviewing said that some bandits had come through the area and were cornered in the woods nearby. They had holed up in the very same cave I used to play around, and were subsequently caught and executed—when they had tried to flee on horseback. He continued that on some nights, people claim to still hear them on their horses, galloping through the woods to the deadly fate that awaited them.

I'm sure glad I didn't hear of the legend when we lived there, or I would never have gotten any sleep. It gives me shivers even now, and I can still hear those horses galloping through the woods in my mind.

CHAPTER 23

A CIGAR-SHAPED UFO

The only thing I can think of that I ever saw that was what I would consider weird was the night my father died, many years ago. I was living and working in a town about an hour and a half away, and that night I had received a call from my mother that my father was in bad shape and wasn't expected to live through the night.

With a great sadness and heaviness, my wife and I got in the car and began the drive out into the country where my parents lived. I had grown up on the same farm where they still lived, but had gone away to college and then stayed in the city to work.

Their place, the old home place as I call it, is way out in the Cumberland Mountains. Back then there weren't any interstate highways, so we had to drive the old curvy state roads that wound through the mountains.

About three-quarters of the way into the drive, we came through the highest part of the mountains and could see the darkened valley below us. I could still see a few lights from the homes down in the valley, but there was one light I spotted across the mountain range that appeared to be behaving strangely.

Finally, it got close enough that I could get a good look at it. It appeared to be going in the same direction as we were traveling, but was several miles off to the left. It wasn't any type of airplane, that much I know. It seemed to be cigar shaped and was moving just above the treetops on the other side of the valley.

All of a sudden, it shot straight up and went completely out of sight. I have never seen anything move that quickly in the sky before. My wife saw it too, so I know my eyes weren't playing tricks on me.

Sadly, when we arrived at the home place, my mother met me out in the yard and informed me that my father had already passed on. Oddly enough, he had died at almost the same time as we had observed the weird object flying over the deep woods of the mountains.

CHAPTER 24

THE SCREAMING WOMAN

I was over on the Kentucky side of the Big South Fork National Park some years ago. It was fall of the year, and I was just out rambling around in the woods, enjoying the peace and solitude of nature.

I had packed a lunch and had spent most of my day enjoying the woods. It had started getting late, so I decided it was time to start hiking my way out. I had just passed one of the many natural waterfalls in the park when I heard a woman scream. It made the short hairs on my neck stand up, it was that bloodcurdling. I stopped walking so I could hear better, but heard nothing but the sounds of the forest. I was almost to the point of wondering if I had imagined the whole thing when I heard the scream again. I carefully began to walk in the direction that I thought the scream came from, even though I wasn't sure I wanted to find the source.

After a few minutes of cautious, quiet walking, I heard it again, but this time it seemed like it was coming from behind me. Rather than try to find out who was screaming, I decided it might be a better idea just to keep going and get out of the woods.

When I got back to the paved lot where I had parked my truck, I saw one of the National Park Service rangers driving by, so I flagged him down and told him what I'd heard.

He didn't seem at all surprised, but told me that he had heard several similar reports recently from other park visitors. He assured me that it most likely wasn't a woman at all, but rather a panther or some other type of large cat, and that I was lucky I got out when I did. He explained that the sounds some of these huge predatory cats make range from that of a woman screaming to a baby crying.

He further stated that since I had first heard the sound in one direction and then behind me, it was possible the big cat could have been stalking me. This scared me even more than the idea of a woman screaming. I haven't been back to the park since and don't know that I'll ever go back alone—I don't want to end up mauled or worse by a hungry panther.

CHAPTER 25

THE GHOSTLY GEESE

The strangest thing I ever had happen to me was when I was working on my daddy's farm in Kentucky, way back when I was just a boy. We raised corn and tobacco, as well as pigs, cows and other livestock. We also had a huge garden far down below the barn, where we raised other vegetables destined for the family dinner table.

Daddy had instructed me to take one of our mules and a wagon out to a certain area down by the creek and fill the wagon full of the rich topsoil that could be found nearby. Kind of disgruntled at such a hard chore, I begrudgingly hitched the mule to the wagon, tossed a shovel in the back, and headed off.

It was a long way down there, and I was feeling kind of lazy that day, so I decided instead to get some rich dirt from a closer place I knew of, about a mile or so closer. It was a huge mound of dirt that looked like it had been there a long time, and I wondered why we had never used it earlier.

I hopped off the wagon, and just about the time I broke into the rich dirt with a shovel, the oddest thing occurred—I heard what sounded like a flock of geese. I stopped and looked up, but didn't see anything in the sky. It was still early in the morning, but there wasn't a cloud in the sky.

I started to dig again, and once again, I heard the geese start up. Mystified, I stopped shoveling and began looking around, trying to find out where the sound was coming from—it wasn't just a few geese, but sounded like a whole huge flock or 'gaggle,' which is the correct term for a group of geese.

Even though the dirt pile backed up to the woods, there were no geese in the trees. Every time I started to dig, the noise seemed to get closer and louder.

Finally, it sounded like they were all around me, very close.

By this point I was spooked and decided to give up on the easy way and go down to the creek and get the dirt like I was told to in the first place. It was a lot of hard, sweaty work, but by lunchtime I had a wagon full of the rich loam my daddy wanted for the garden.

When I got back, he met me at the garden with another shovel and, thankfully, helped me unload the wagon. As we shoveled the dirt into the garden, I sort of told on myself and mentioned that I had started to get the dirt from another place until the sound of geese had scared me away.

My father stopped shoveling and gave me a very stern look. "Don't ever dig in that mound of dirt again," he stated solemnly. "That's an Indian burial mound, and it would be disrespectful to disturb them."

I was both shocked and shamed. To this day, I believe the noises I heard were the spirits of the Native Americans warning me that they did not want their resting place disturbed.

CHAPTER 26

THE BLACK DOG

I was just a child when this happened, about ten or so, but I've never forgotten it and I never will. It was in the fall of the year, so it would have been early October. I believe it was just a few days before Halloween. We had gone up into Ohio to visit my grandmother, who still lived on the family farm after my grandfather had passed away the year before.

I was out wandering around in the huge yard and decided to go for a stroll through the cornfield adjacent to the yard. Now, if you've never seen a cornfield in Ohio or Indiana, these can be massive, covering many, many acres.

The ears of corn had already been harvested, and I was having a grand time walking through the dead stalks that had yet to be plowed under. I remember it seeming spooky, like that Stephen King movie *Children of the Corn*. Heck, I half expected Bigfoot to pop out from between the rows.

After what seemed like miles (but was probably only a quarter mile or so), I came out of either the back or the side of the cornfield (I had been running around like a wild ape and wasn't sure which way was which at this point—the rows all look the same after a while if you're a kid and not paying attention).

I didn't see the farmhouse anywhere, so instead had the not-so-bright idea to head into the woods.

If I had found the cornfield confusing, then the woods were a hundred times more so, at least. I was a smart-aleck suburban kid (we lived on a cul-de-sac, for crying out loud) who thought he knew everything there was to know about the woods. Boy, was I ever in for a surprise.

I was just moseying along, looking at rocks and trees and birds and squirrels, when I noticed it was starting to get dark. It was already kind of dark in the woods anyway, but I hadn't noticed the quickly setting sun, so it would be really, really dark soon.

Instead of panicking, I did have at least enough sense to keep my head about me and ignore the urge to just start running in any particular direction.

Although now I know that the best thing to do if you're lost in the woods is to stay in one place (otherwise you'll end up walking in circles without even realizing it), I decided to hike my way out of the woods. I had no idea which way the farm or the main road or anything was, so I just picked a direction and started walking.

It was completely pitch black in the woods. I didn't have any kind of light with me, of course, and I couldn't see any lights anywhere in the distance. I just kept walking and finally sat down beneath a huge tree and wept. I was truly, absolutely lost in the woods.

After I had been sitting for probably fifteen minutes or so, I stopped crying and decided to get up and start walking again. As I continued to make my way through the maze of trees and dense brush, I heard a sound off to my right.

Thinking it might be someone looking for me, I called out. No response came, but I could hear the noises getting closer.

A couple of minutes later, the biggest dog I have ever seen poked his massive head out of the bush. This dog was immense, like a Labrador but even bigger.

Looking back, it may have been a mastiff or some kind of Great Dane hybrid.

At first I was sure the huge beast was going to eat me—or at least tear me to shreds—and at that point, I almost didn't care. Instead, the dog walked right over to me and, while wagging his massive tail, licked my hand. I petted him for a few minutes and was amazed at how beautiful he was. He wasn't wearing a collar, but he looked healthy and very clean. His coat was soft and shiny, not ragged and full of burrs and ticks like you might find on a dog roaming in the woods.

I began walking again—at least now I had some company. The dog eventually began walking in front of me, and every few feet would stop and look back, as if urging me to keep following him. I was so tired that all I wanted to do was find a place to sit down, but it was really getting chilly now in the dark, so I did the best I could to keep the dog in sight and kept moving.

After what seemed like an hour, we stepped out of the woods onto a paved road.

Civilization at last! However, I wasn't sure whether to follow the road to the left or to the right. I looked at the dog, and as if he understood my predicament, he started trotting off down the blacktop to the left. I figured it was a fifty-fifty shot anyway, so I continued following him.

There were still no houses or lights in sight, but the night was clear enough that I could follow the dog, which was following the road. I did find it kind of strange that he didn't stop and sniff things every few feet like most dogs do, but I was too tired to care.

Soon, I began to see some lights off in the distance. It looked like houses, so I hoped I had gone in the right direction. As I continued along, still following the dog, I saw a pair of automobile headlights approaching in the distance. I almost started to hide in case it was some kind of weird stranger, but instead decided to stay by the road, but got safely off onto the shoulder. The dog stood by my side, waiting.

As the vehicle drew nearer, I recognized it as my uncle's dilapidated old Buick. I was rescued!

The car pulled over and my dad jumped out. He was thankful to see me, as I had been gone for hours and no one knew where I was. He said they had been out for the last couple of hours driving the back roads looking for me, while some of my cousins had gone into the woods, and another batch had headed over to a nearby lake.

Once I assured him I was okay, I piled into the back seat and fell fast asleep, enjoying the warmth of the Buick's heater. I don't even remember arriving back at the house, as my dad had carried me inside and put me to bed.

The next morning over breakfast, all the conversation was about my little adventure the night before. I told the whole story about becoming lost and how the big black dog had led me out of the woods and in the right direction towards the house. I asked both my dad and uncle if they hadn't seen the dog waiting beside me when they stopped in the car, but neither one had any idea what I was talking about—they hadn't seen any dog, just a tired, cold boy standing and shivering on the side of the road.

My uncle asked around, and no one had ever seen or heard of such a large black dog being owned by anyone in the area.

And this was the type of farming community that was pretty tight-knit—everyone knew everyone else.

I often wonder if maybe I even imagined the dog, but a part of me knows better—I remember what his tongue felt like when he licked my hand, and how soft and warm his coat felt when I stroked him. Maybe the dog was some sort of guardian angel—I suppose an angel could take on any form, and I would have been a lot more scared of a strange person than a big black dog. Either way, he led me out of the woods, and I'll never forget.

CHAPTER 27

THE GLOWING BALL

I had been over to visit a friend from school who lived nearby. We lived in a semirural area, so in this case 'nearby' meant about three and a half miles by road. I had originally ridden my bicycle over, but when it came time to go home, I was tired and thought I would walk back through the woods. Being in the country, the roads were very hilly, and I felt too tired to ride my bike all the way back. By cutting through the woods in a more or less straight line, I could cut the distance by more than half. I would just leave my bike overnight, as I was planning on going back the next day anyway.

I told my friend goodbye and struck off through the woods toward home. It was already getting dark, but I didn't really mind. I had taken the shortcut through the woods many times before and knew the route like the back of my hand. I had cleared the first wooded area and entered a large open field (it had once been a cow pasture, but was now just a huge expanse overgrown with weeds), when something caught my eye.

On the other side of the field, perhaps a quarter mile or so away, the area was once again heavily forested. Right at the edge of the field I observed what I can only describe as a large ball of light, about the size of a basketball. It sort of pulsated between orange and red in color. It wasn't really bright, but bright enough that I could see that it lit up the lower parts of the trees that were near it.

At first, I had assumed maybe it was someone with a large flashlight or maybe even a lantern, but as I got closer, I observed that I could see all the way around and even partially through the ball of light. It slowly and gently bobbed along right at the edge of the forest at a varying height I estimated to be about seven to ten feet off the ground. It was totally noiseless and seemed to travel at a consistent speed forward.

I had stopped walking while I observed the ball of light, but decided to try to go in for a closer look—for some reason, at the time it never occurred to me to be scared. As I got to within approximately thirty yards of the light, it shot almost straight up and disappeared over the treetops and into the woods. I waited around for a few minutes to see if it might reappear, but it unfortunately did not.

At that point I started to get a little spooked and decided I'd rather not go through the woods after all. Instead, I went back to my friend's house and retrieved my bicycle to ride home. I guess the sighting of the ball of light gave me a little adrenaline surge, as I no longer felt too tired to bike home and was too spooked to venture through the woods.

I never did see the light again, despite many attempts at looking for it. I did, however, hear similar stories from people in the area who had seen something almost identical at various times.

CHAPTER 28

IT WAS...A PIZZA?

I got one that's kinda funny, but weird at the same time, and totally from the realm of the unexplained. My friend Jake and I had gone hiking in the infamous New Jersey Pine Barrens, home of the Jersey Devil, among other things.

Now there's not really that much to see in the Pine Barrens, except for pine trees—I guess that's why they call it the barrens. But it is a really creepy place, what with all the legends of monsters, mobsters, KKK, devil worshipers and whatnot. It's one of those places where you always feel like you're being watched...And truth be known, you probably are!

So anyway, I was visiting my friend in New Jersey, and he had promised to show me the infamous Pine Barrens, so there we were. It was on a Saturday, and we seemed to have the place all to ourselves. Jake parked his truck in a turnout on the side of a dirt road (really just what we would call a cow path down south) and off we went.

I admit, it was a very spooky, eerie-feeling place. Of course my head was full of legends about monsters and disposed bodies of mob hits and the like. We had hiked maybe a mile or so into the barrens when we came across the strangest thing we would see on the whole trip. It was a pizza!

Yes, that's right, a pizza. A whole pizza, cooked and sliced but still whole, just sitting on the ground. There was no box around, nor any other evidence of anyone having been or currently being nearby. The pizza looked fresh, like it couldn't have been there more than a few hours, tops. We half jokingly dared each other to have a slice, each eventually concluding there wasn't enough money in the world to get us to eat the pizza.

Sadly, I didn't have a camera with me, or I would have taken a picture of it.

It boggles the mind. How did it get there? Why was it there? Was it laced with drugs? Or maybe a trap laid by the Jersey Devil? I reached the conclusion that I had seen enough of the Pine Barrens and was happy to leave by this point. And just for the record, it was a large-sized pie with pepperoni and a thin crust.

CHAPTER 29

DEVIL WORSHIP CAVE

My friends and I heard of a cave over in Blount County, not too far from the Great Smoky Mountains National Park, that was supposedly a site where devil worshipers and/or Satanists met on a regular basis. One Friday night, we decided we were brave enough to check it out. My one friend, Stanley, had family that lived in the area, and he knew pretty much where the cave was, so it was decided we would make his aunt's house our base camp for this expedition into the bizarre.

We arrived at her house just before dark and started getting our gear together. There were four of us in all, including myself, Stanley, and a couple of girls whom we had coaxed into tagging along (I won't name their names just in case they might see this). It was in October, a couple of weeks before Halloween, so Stanley and I thought a spooky trip like this might be a good way to get to know the girls a little better, if you get my meaning. Walking around exploring a spooky cave with scared, beautiful girls clinging onto us for dear life sounded like a great night to Stanley and me!

We gathered up a few glow sticks, several yards of rope, and some snacks and liquid refreshment (hey, the drinking age was eighteen at that time in Tennessee, so we were legal!) and headed off into the woods.

We had to walk quite a ways just to get to the farm the cave was on, so the whole way Stanley and I were telling all these wild stories about ghosts and witches and hooded figures and such—we were really playing it up for the benefit of the girls, who by this point were probably having second thoughts about tagging along, yet they were too scared to turn around and try to find the way back by themselves in the dark. Our plan was working just as we expected!

After nearly getting lost (and not on purpose) a couple of times, Stanley was finally able to locate the entrance to the cave. I'll admit one thing, it was sure isolated—I began to wonder if all those creepy stories and legends we had heard at school might be true after all!

We cracked our glow sticks and ventured inside, the girls clinging to us as planned. Once inside, the cave was much like a labyrinth, with all kinds of twists and turns. One of the other nicknames I had heard the cave called was Rescue Squad Cave, due to all the people who had allegedly gotten lost inside over the years, and it was easy to see why—every passage seemed to look just alike.

Shortly, we saw some light ahead, and when we stepped around the corner, we found evidence of some kind of strange ceremony. There was a large pentagram drawn on one wall of the chamber, along with some other strange symbols.

There were candles that were still burning sitting on either side of the pentagram. We stood quietly and listened for the sound of anyone else moving around, but the silence was deafening. We slowly and carefully turned around and started back the way we had come in.

After a couple of false starts, wrong turns and almost stepping off a huge drop-off, we finally made our way back out of the cave entrance. Outside, we could hear what sounded like chanting begin to echo from inside the cave.

Although Stanley and I were spooked, we were doing our best not to show it. By this point the girls were begging us to leave, so it was decided it was past time to leave.

That was my one and only trek to Devil Worship Cave, and as far as I know, neither Stanley nor the girls—understandably—ever ventured back.

At least we were able to confirm all the tales we had heard in school were true, and were smart enough to realize there are some things and places better left alone.

CHAPTER 30

BROWN MOUNTAIN LIGHTS

At the time, I was living in Mountain City, Tennessee, which is in the extreme northeastern corner of the state, right on the border with Virginia and North Carolina. My aunt and her husband decided one weekend that they would like to drive over into North Carolina and try to see if we could see the legendary Brown Mountain Lights.

It was only a couple of hours' drive, so we loaded up the van and headed out, eventually parking at an overpass along a dirt road and then hiking the rest of the way in to a spot that overlooked Linville Gorge, with Brown Mountain on the other side. We arrived just before sundown, set up our supplies at a spot with a good view of the mountain, and settled in for the night.

Shortly after dark, the show began. I had heard about the lights all my life, but this was my first time ever seeing them. Some of the lights were sort of an off-white, but many of them were also faintly colored red, blue, green and orange. Some of the lights even seemed to change colors as they flitted about the mountain, some in the trees and some over the tops of the trees in all directions.

The most amazing lights I saw were the ones that appeared to be among the trees on the mountainside. These lights were similar in brightness to a fluorescent lantern and seemed to be moving laterally through the trees with great speed.

They would wink out and then reappear at a spot probably a couple of miles away. From our vantage point, it looked like someone running through the woods while switching an electric lantern off and on.

The next morning when observing the terrain where we had seen the lights, it was obviously impossible that it could have been anyone with a lantern—the area was craggy, almost sheer cliff faces!

We went back on several occasions afterward and were always treated to a spectacular light show. These lights have been seen for centuries, and there are many legends about them, which you can find online with a quick search.

Many scientists and geologists have also studied the phenomenon, but have never been able to fully explain the lights.

If you want to observe a possible paranormal mystery, I highly recommend visiting Brown Mountain, North Carolina. In my experience, late summer and early fall are the best times to see the lights.

CHAPTER 31

THE GIANT BALL OF ICE

Once when I was a kid, one of our cows had gotten out and taken off into the woods somewhere. My dad tasked me with finding it and bringing it home, so the next morning at daybreak, I grabbed a piece of rope and took off through the woods in the direction where the cow was last seen. She had a bell on her neck, so I figured she wouldn't be too awful hard to find.

I covered all of the cornfield, where I thought she might be gorging herself, and then followed the woods down toward a spring branch that ran through our property. The spring wasn't that deep, and I thought she might have gone down there for a drink or even be bathing herself in the cold water.

Shortly, I heard the dull sound of her cowbell and, sure enough, found her at the edge of the creek, standing in the water up over her hooves. She seemed surprised to see me, and I had no trouble getting close enough to get the rope around her neck and start leading her back toward the house.

I had enjoyed this particular little chore, as it had gotten me out of doing some of the much harder chores on the farm, so I decided to take my time going back and take the long way around. I liked being out in the woods and just wanted to give myself a little more enjoyment—my idea of my reward for finding the cow.

As we followed along the creek, headed back toward the house, I heard something crashing through the woods. The cow heard it too, and she stopped in her tracks and let out a small bellow. I listened carefully and didn't hear anything else, but started up through the woods where I had heard the noise.

About a hundred yards into the woods, I found what had made the noise. It was a huge ball of ice, about half the size of a large washtub. It had obviously fallen from above, as I could see freshly broken tree limbs and branches up above it. It appeared to have come in at a slight angle.

It reminded me of a hailstone, but was bigger than any I had ever heard tell of. A good portion of it had broken off and was melting into the forest floor.

I hurried on home at that point and told my dad about it, and we went back for another look. However, most of it had already melted by that time, although it was still ten times bigger than any hail I had ever seen.

It was a clear day, in the summertime, so I don't think it was giant hail. I hadn't heard any airplane pass over, either. We never did figure out where it came from.

CHAPTER 32

THE GRINNING MAN

When I was a child, my parents and my little sister and I would often go visit my grandparents who lived on a farm in West Virginia. At the time, we lived in the suburbs of a large city, so it was a refreshing change of pace for all of us to get out into the country for a bit.

I always loved visiting my grandparents, and was free to roam about the woods bordering their farm to my heart's content. There were ponds, a creek or two, and lots and lots of places to explore.

One morning, while out looking for berries or wildflowers in the woods, I caught sight of a man standing inside the trees. He looked harmless enough, but it was kind of creepy because he had a huge grin on his face.

I kept on walking along, trying not to pay him any attention, but he just stood in the same spot and continued grinning. Now this was back in the days before 'stranger danger' and all that, but looking back, I should have taken off then and there. Instead, I tried to stare him down.

No matter what I did, he just stood there, motionless, with that weird grin on his face. I eventually tried waving at him, but this elicited no response. I tired of the game after about fifteen minutes or so and eventually made my way back to my grand-parents' house.

When I got in, I told my grandma about the grinning man, and she became visibly upset. She went and got my grandpa and told him about what I had seen.

Grandpa went into the bedroom and got his shotgun and headed off in the direction of the woods where I had been. He stated very vehemently that nobody had any business being on their property, especially when his granddaughters were nearby.

I got kind of scared when we heard a couple of shotgun blasts a few minutes later—I was afraid grandpa had killed someone. I went and hid in the back bedroom.

However, when he came back inside later, he let us know that he hadn't seen a soul, but fired off a couple of rounds to make sure the grinning stranger knew he wasn't welcome here.

After that little incident, I never did venture too far into the woods anymore when we went to visit. It scares me more to think about it now than it did when I was a child.

CHAPTER 33

THE MYSTERIOUS MONKEY

The weirdest thing that I ever came across in the woods was a monkey. It wasn't anything big, like a chimp or a gorilla, but it was a monkey, I'm just not sure what kind—maybe a capuchin or a spider monkey since it was small.

I was hunting deer in Alabama with some cousins, and I was up a tree, hoping that a big buck might come along. The birds were all upset, however, and thrashing about in the trees, so I was afraid they were making too much noise and would scare the deer off.

I was trying to see what was upsetting the birds, when I heard an odd noise.

It kind of sounded like a bird, but not a regular wild bird, it sounded more like a parrot or something exotic. Scanning the treetops with my binoculars, I finally spotted what was making the odd noises. It was a small monkey.

I had a clear shot at him, but I just didn't feel right shooting a monkey. He seemed almost human. Plus, I wasn't sure if it was legal or not, and I didn't want to get into any trouble with the game warden.

Instead, I tried calling it. It looked in my direction, but never would come any closer than a tree or two over from me. I took a handful of trail mix out of my jacket and threw it on the ground below, and eventually the monkey came over and ate part of it before scampering off into the woods. If it had gotten close enough, I would have liked to have tried catching it and making it a pet, but I would have also been afraid of it, as monkeys are known to carry tuberculosis and possibly even rabies.

I never did see it again, and around the fire that night the guys accused me of having been drinking, but I promise that I hadn't had a drop. What a monkey was doing out in the woods in Alabama, I haven't a clue. Near as I can figure, it was probably an escaped research animal or had been someone's pet at one time.

We still hunt the area in season, but I have yet to see the monkey again, and it's going on five years now since my sighting.

CHAPTER 34

THE RIVER GAME

My strangest encounter in the woods was one time during deer season. I was sitting in a blind, waiting for a deer, when I heard some sort of commotion in the woods. Lots of noise, branches breaking, it sounded a lot bigger than a deer.

What I saw still amazes me to this day. First, I saw a lot of squirrel and chipmunks pass by. Then some raccoons and rabbits followed. Then came a bunch of deer, a whole herd of them, running like mad. I was too stunned at what I had just witnessed to even try to get off a shot.

I've heard stories like this before and was afraid the animals might be running from a forest fire, so I decided to go in the same direction as the 'river of game' I had just seen pass by.

On my way back to the truck, I passed some other hunters and stopped to talk.

They had seen the same thing that I had, and were just as at a loss to explain it. They, too, were so stunned that it didn't occur to them to take a shot at any of the bucks.

We looked around for a while, but didn't see any evidence of a forest fire or anything else. I stopped at a ranger station and let them know what we'd seen.

They double-checked to make sure there weren't any fires in the area, but everything reported back clear.

I've since heard the suggestion that, among other things, a bear or large cat may have been on the prowl in the area and spooked all the smaller animals.

Another guy suggested there might have been a forthcoming earthquake in the area. That would make sense, sort of, and some research online does indeed indicate animals will sometimes flee ahead of a quake; however, there was never any earthquake in the area that I could find. Beats me!

CHAPTER 35

THE ABANDONED CAB

When I was a teenager, some friends and I had gone exploring on federal land.

I won't name the place, because I'm pretty sure we were trespassing. Let's just say it was way out in the middle of absolute nowhere, and leave it at that.

We were just goofing off, drinking some beers, having a good time far away from prying eyes. We had been walking through a power cut, but decided to stray off into the woods for a while.

Again, I want to stress just how far out this place was. We were miles and miles from any semblance of a road or highway. Making our way through the woods was difficult at best, and many times we had to hike around areas that were overgrown too thickly to pass.

We eventually found a little clearing beneath a stand of pine trees and sat down to take a break for a while. One of the guys with us, I'll call him Andy, was horsing around, tossing big rocks off into the trees and getting a kick out of hearing them crash through the brush below.

However, one particular rock didn't go crashing down the hill through the trees, but instead hit something heavy, making a dull metallic sound. We all got quiet real fast, trying to figure out what on earth he might have hit. We waited a few minutes, and then Andy tossed another hand-sized rock in the same general direction. Again, we heard it strike something metallic. Time to go explore and find out what was up here with us.

Making our way down the steep embankment into a ravine, we jokingly came up with all manner of imaginative scenarios, including a UFO, a moonshine still, and a plane crash. Oddly enough, what we found was just about as weird and farfetched. At the bottom of the ravine, resting on its side, was the ancient, rusting hulk of an abandoned taxicab.

Rust was about all that was holding it together, but we could still make out the fare amount painted on the door, but not the name of the cab company.

Based on the body shape of the car, we guessed it to be from the 1930s or 1940s. All the windows were smashed out and the license plates were nowhere to be seen, so we had no idea where it could have come from and how it could have possibly ended up there.

We cautiously crept up far enough to have a look inside, half expecting to find a dead body or two, but nothing other than the rotting interior of the car could be seen. It's probably still there to this day, but like I said, you'd probably be trespassing if you went to see it, so for now the location will have to remain a mystery, just like the cab and how it came to rest deep in the woods of Ohio.

CHAPTER 36

THE MAN IN THE WELL

This happened when we were kids, my brother and I. We were only a year apart, so if memory serves correct, we would have been about nine and ten years old respectively. Deep in the woods, a couple of miles or so from where we lived, was an old abandoned farm. Other than a crumbling foundation and a dangerously leaning chimney, no trace of the farmhouse that had once stood on the property remained.

Near the foundation was an old well or cistern, where the folks who lived there had most likely caught rainwater. The cistern was covered with several half-rotten boards, but we knew to stay far away from it—abandoned wells are dangerous, and if you fell in, you could easily break a leg or even drown.

Well, on this particular trip out past the old farm, we noticed that the boards were missing from the top of the cistern, and the rock-lined hole was wide open. We knew not to get too close, but curiosity got the best of the both of us, and we just had to have a look down into the deep, dark hole. We figured some wild animal or maybe even someone's livestock might have ventured on top of the boards and had fallen in.

For fear of standing too close and having the side collapse (these wells or cisterns were dug by hand and also hand-lined with smooth river rock), we instead lay down and crawled up to the edge to have a peek.

My brother got to the edge about a second or two before I did, and I heard him gasp with surprise. His eyes were as wide as saucers and his mouth hung open. I eased up to the lip to have a look for myself—and I nearly jumped out of my skin when I saw a body about twelve feet below, floating headfirst in the brackish water. We jumped up and ran as fast as we could back home, both of us too shocked to even speak as we beat a path back to the house.

Once we had arrived home safely, we caught our breath and located my uncle Pete, who just happened to be the only adult home at the time. I say 'adult' because he was older than us, but I'm sure in reality he was probably only sixteen or seventeen years old at the time. We told him of our discovery, and even though he threatened to pound us if we were telling lies, he could tell we were really scared. He got a length of rope from the storage shed, and we all trekked through the woods to the abandoned farm.

Upon arrival, sure enough, Pete peered in and saw the man in the well. My brother and I held our breath as Pete tied a loop in the rope and managed to snag one of the boots. We even helped Pete pull on the rope to bring the body up and out of the well.

As the body was near the top, I shut my eyes tight. The only dead person I'd ever seen was in a funeral home, and I was afraid I'd have nightmares after seeing a bloated corpse pulled from a well.

All of a sudden, Pete let loose with a string of curse words that I'm sure turned the air around us blue. I opened my eyes just a crack as he turned the body over—it was a dummy! It looked almost like some farmer's scarecrow, but whoever had made it had taken great pains to make sure it looked real.

Relieved that it wasn't a real body, we took a closer look at the dummy. It was wearing faded blue denim overalls, a plaid shirt, and worn work boots. The head was fashioned out of a dried gourd with drawn-on eyes and a crude slit for a mouth, and it had an old hunting cap shoved down over the top of it.

Looking back, someone spent a lot of time putting it together and filling it with straw.

At first, Pete blamed us and was ready to give us the pounding he'd promised if we were making it up. We assured him we had no part in it, and he seemed to believe it—at least he didn't beat us up.

I guess the real mystery was why someone would go to all that trouble—no one lived for miles around, and we had only happened upon the elaborate prank by chance. Pete tore the dummy to pieces on the spot and swore into the neighboring woods in case the merry pranksters were watching from a distance.

We covered the cistern with some more old boards and a few large tree limbs for good measure, and that was the end of it.

Pretty weird.

CHAPTER 37

DEVIL DOLL

Several years ago, my husband and I bought an old, renovated farmhouse in North Georgia. Having been apartment dwellers previously, it was so nice to have our own place with a yard and trees and all.

One day, only a couple of weeks after we had moved in, I was out in the expanse of woods that adjoined our property, looking for wildflowers to dry and make arrangements for our new house.

While tramping around in one particular area, I rounded a corner and found what must have been someone's garbage dump from years gone by. There were lots of old bottles and rusted-out cans—I even gathered a few of the bottles to clean up and display around the house, lending an air of authenticity to my 'shabby chic' decor.

I went back to the dump site on several occasions, and on one particular trip I noticed something odd resting in some vines at the base of a huge oak tree.

Reaching in carefully, I was amazed to pull out an old bisque doll's head. The fabric had long since rotted away, but after a bit of digging, I was also able to find the fragile arms and legs for the doll.

Amazed with my find, I hurried back to the house and set about sewing a body for the doll, to make her whole again. Once finished, I placed her on the ornate fireplace mantel in our living room. She looked right at home up there.

That night was when things started getting weird. Just as we were falling asleep, I thought I heard the sound of giggling and a rapping noise coming from downstairs. I roused my husband, but he assured me it was just the wind or raccoons in the garbage or something, and rolled over and went back to sleep.

Throughout the night, I would doze off only to be awakened by little noises from downstairs.

Finally, I had had enough and got out of bed myself. I put on a housecoat and crept down the stairs with a flashlight. As I shined the light around the living room, I was startled to see the doll sitting on the floor beside the fireplace. I assumed it had fallen, but I was literally dumbstruck at how it could have fallen four feet from the mantel and landed in a sitting position on the far side of the mantel without breaking the head or limbs. I replaced the doll and went back to bed, but continued to hear noises throughout the night.

The next morning when I got up, I went downstairs to start breakfast and was startled to see the doll once again sitting on the floor next to the fireplace. I picked up the doll and, while examining it for any cracks, noticed how evil the expression on its face appeared. Something didn't feel right. I'll admit that I was more than a little bit scared at the time.

After breakfast, I took the doll back out into the woods and replaced it where I had found the head and limbs. I slept soundly that night, and every night thereafter. We've lived here for almost twenty years now, and I've never experienced anything even slightly out of the ordinary. There are some things that can't be explained and times when it is best to leave well enough alone.

I learned my lesson about bringing things into the house from out in the woods, and if I ever see another doll out there, I'm going to run as fast as I can in the other direction.

CHAPTER 38

TAROT OF THE WOODS

The strangest thing I ever encountered in the woods was in the Jefferson National Forest, not too far off the Appalachian Trail.

I had made a day trip to the forest to do some hiking, mainly just to get out and get some exercise. The Appalachian Trail cuts through the edge of the area, and there are some beautiful hiking spots. It was a fine spring day, just a little bit of morning chill in the woods, and I felt lucky to have the place to myself.

I had wandered off the main trail on to a smaller, but well-marked side trail, when I noticed a tarot card nailed to a tree, maybe thirty yards or so off into the woods. I walked up to the tree to have a better look, finding it kind of odd. The card was still stiff and new looking, so I gather it hadn't been there for very long. I found it to be strange, but have spent enough time in the woods to know that sometimes you come across some pretty weird things. As I turned to go, I spotted another tarot card nailed to a tree yet farther off in the distance. I walked over to it, as well.

Same thing, new-looking card, nailed to a tree with a single roofing nail. I scanned around the woods and saw another card a little distance off. I went and had a look at that one too. Every time I spotted a new card and went to have a look, I would see another off in the distance. I followed the 'trail' as far as twelve cards, then kind of got the heebie-jeebies and decided maybe I didn't need to go any deeper into the woods.

I hiked back out to the main trail I had been on and didn't see anyone else or have any further strange incidents. I have no idea what the meaning of the tarot cards was, why they were nailed to trees seemingly at random intervals or what the cards would have eventually led me to, but not being armed at all, save for a small pocketknife, I wasn't in the mood to find out.

CHAPTER 39

OUIJA WEIRDNESS

When I was a kid, I was not allowed to have a Ouija board in the house. I found that out the hard way when I borrowed one from a friend of mine from school, and my mom had an absolute fit when I brought it in. I sheepishly took it back to the owner and kind of forgot about it. I was no longer tempted to mess with the unknown.

Fast-forward years later, and I was out in the woods bowhunting. I had climbed up to the top of a draw and was hoping to spot a nice deer to take down. Off to one side, I saw the remains of someone's campsite. Now keep in mind, this wasn't a normal camping area by any stretch of the imagination. We're talking extremely rugged terrain, miles and miles from anywhere. The going is so rough, you need either a horse or an ATV with high clearance to even make it to the base camp area.

Nonetheless, here was an abandoned campsite. There were shredded remnants of a heavy tarp someone had used to make a lean-to, some trash, and a stone circle where a fire had been made. Sitting in the middle of the stone circle, of all things, was a Ouija board. It was singed around the edges, as if someone had tried to burn it in the fire, but it hadn't fully caught ablaze. I picked it up and looked it over.

I guess maybe it was because of how my mom had berated me for bring one into our house, telling me how evil they were, but I got really creeped out. One of the legends about the boards I had heard growing up was that you couldn't burn one unless you snapped it in half first. And here in my hand was proof—the back side of the board was blackened with soot, and the corners and edges were singed, but it hadn't burned.

I carefully placed the board back into the stone fire circle and hurried off to another part of the woods. The next year when I was hunting in the same area, I plucked up enough courage to visit the campsite again, but this time the Ouija board was nowhere to be found. Call me superstitious if you want, but why take a chance with something like that? Not me.

CHAPTER 40

VOODOO RITUAL

I'll tell you about something weird that I came across in the woods one time in the Pocono Mountains. I was just a kid at the time and was spending part of my summer vacation in the mountains with my mom and dad.

We were staying in a rustic cabin way back in the hills, and I was having a grand time exploring the woods. I was raised in the city, in a suburb of Philly, so it was a nice change of pace to see trees and nature.

I had wandered a good distance from the cabin one day, looking for wildflowers. I was following a little trail and noticed what looked like a small cave up the hill to my left. Feeling adventurous, I climbed the steep bank to have a look inside.

When I got to the area I had seen from below, I was disappointed to find that it wasn't actually a cave, but more of a hollowed-out little stone ledge about halfway up the steep embankment.

Peering inside the little shelf, I was shocked to see what

looked like a little homemade doll. On closer inspection, I noticed that it appeared to have been crudely fashioned from burlap, with a small shock of human-looking hair at the top, and buttons for eyes. There were also straight pins sticking into it—I suddenly realized that I was looking at a voodoo doll. I had read about creepy stuff in books in the library, but had never seen anything quite like this.

There were some other items on the ledge, including a mostly burned candle, a small china saucer with some objects in it, and a piece of parchment rolled up and tied with twine. About that time, a stark realization began to creep over me.

I suddenly got goose pimples all over my whole body—I had stumbled across someone's voodoo ritual. I carefully made my way back down the bank, trying hard not to leave any trace that I'd been up there, and went straight back to our cabin.

For the three more days or so we stayed in the Poconos, I refused to venture out of sight of our cabin, afraid I might have been observed sticking my nose where it didn't belong. I even had trouble sleeping at night, every little creak and groan of the forest sending me into spasms of fear that a voodoo priestess was coming to get me.

My mom and dad asked me what was wrong, and I just played sick, saying I didn't feel like going out into the woods. I was very happy when the time came to go back home to Philly. I never did tell them what I found, and I've never mentioned it to another soul until now.

I never had any bad luck or anything after the incident, so I guess I didn't upset anything. Who would have ever imagined there were voodoo practitioners in the Pocono Mountains, of all places?

CHAPTER 41

THE BURIED SUITCASE

I was out in the woods scouting deer, in anticipation of the opening of bow season in a couple of weeks. It was a good way to spend the weekend, I figured, and would hopefully increase my chances of getting a nice trophy buck for the wall of my den at home. I'd already found some good, likely spots to place a tree stand, and was on my way back to my four-wheeler when I decided to sit down beneath a tree and take a rest.

As I sat down, I put my hand on a large flat rock that was at the base of the tree. The rock wobbled and rocked a little bit, and I heard a hollow-sounding thunking noise coming from underneath. Curiosity up, I scraped leaves from around the rock, and once exposed, I found I had no trouble rolling it over to one side and out of the way.

Underneath the stone, I found that the soil was loose, and it was obvious someone had previously been digging here. I looked around and found a pretty good-sized stick and started scraping away the dirt. Much to my surprise, a square outline began to take shape. Using my gloved hands, I had soon uncovered the top of an aluminum case of some sort.

I cleared some more dirt from around the sides and very soon had made the hole big enough that I was able to grasp the dirt-encrusted handle and lift the case free. I was surprised at the heft of it, and I could feel something shift inside. It was one of those aluminum flight cases and had been locked with a key. As visions of buried cash and jewels danced in my head, I grabbed the Leatherman tool from the pouch on my belt and went to work on the locks.

About fifteen minutes later, I finally broke through the second lock. I held my breath as I slowly opened the case, already thinking what I would do with all the cash I was about to find (or at least the reward money if it turned out to be stolen).

Inside was a pillowcase and a laminated note. The note was actually a poem dedicated to Brewster, the Best Bird-Dog Ever. I felt the pillowcase with my gloved hand, just to make sure. Yep, he'd been in the ground for quite some time, and I felt the unmistakable feel of bones without having to open the pillow-case, which was tied shut with a short length of nylon rope.

I thought of the many good hunting dogs I'd owned over the years, and I admired the tenacity of anyone who would lug their deceased dog in a suitcase all the way out here in the middle of nowhere. What better tribute than to bury the dog in the same area where fond hunting memories were once made?

Satisfied, I carefully reburied the case, replaced the rock and covered it with leaves, all the while with tears in my eyes. I may not have found any loot, but instead found a real treasure—there's nothing like a good canine hunting companion.

Sorry to have disturbed you, Brewster—I hope you're having a blast flushing grouse out of the brush in dog heaven.

CHAPTER 42

THE IMPRISONED TOAD

The strangest thing I ever came across in the woods happened during deer season when I was out hunting in Catoosa. [Author's Note: Catoosa is a Tennessee Wildlife Management Area where hunting is allowed in season.]

I had been up in my tree stand since before daylight and hadn't had any luck, so I figured I'd climb down and stretch my legs for a bit. I was starting to stiffen up from sitting in the tree for so long.

Catoosa has been a popular hunting destination for centuries, long before the white man ever came to America. As such, people unthinkingly leave a lot of trash in the woods. I was always taught that if you take it in, you take it back out, and not to leave any trash for the next fellow. Some people don't grasp that concept and leave trash strewn all over the forest.

When I'm out hunting, I'll often pick up cans or bottles and stuff left behind by thoughtless hunters, just because I like the idea of leaving nature better than when I found it.

This time, while I was walking about having my stretch, I happened to notice the neck of a half-buried soda bottle sticking out of the ground. I reached down and gave it a tug, and it easily pulled free of the dirt and leaves.

It was one of those old Coca-Cola bottles, the kind made of thick, greenish glass. I was just about to put it in my pack when I noticed what looked like mud and leaves inside the bottle. When I tried to shake the gunk out, so as not to mess up my pack, I heard a funny noise. I looked around, didn't see anything, but then I heard it again. About that time, I felt something move—inside the bottle!

I almost dropped it, thinking it might be a snake, but on closer inspection—I couldn't believe what I was seeing—there was a frog or a toad of some sort trapped inside the bottle! I got the bottle angled around to where I could see a little better, and sure enough, I could peek into the bottle and see the frog looking back at me. It was a pretty tight fit for the little guy, he didn't even have enough room to turn around.

I took the bottle back to camp, and that evening showed the other guys I was hunting with what I had found. One of my friends, Dan, helped me carefully break the bottle so we could free the frog. After we got it out, it sat there for a few minutes and then took off hopping through the woods. I'm sure it was happy to be set free.

The only answer we could come up with was that the frog had ventured inside the bottle when it was small (maybe even a tadpole) and had thought he had a good place to hole up for cold weather. The bottle had been tilted in the ground at such an angle that he had enough water, and I suppose, enough to eat— he wasn't exactly fat, but was fat enough to not be able to fit back out the narrow bottle opening. I can't imagine how many weeks or even months he may have been trapped inside.

I ended up not getting a deer that trip, but my story of the toad in the bottle continues to be told and retold year after year, so all in all it was worth it. I'm just glad I found the little guy before he either drowned or starved in his glass prison.

CHAPTER 43

THE OPENED GRAVES

Back when I used to hunt quite a bit, there was an old cemetery way off back in the woods close to Jefferson City. Most of the stones were so old and weathered that you couldn't make out the names or dates. From what I recall, the ones you could read dated back to the early 1800s.

I had passed the cemetery on many occasions and never gave it much thought.

One time though, when I passed by, something out of the ordinary had happened.

All the graves, every one of them, had been dug up. I was stymied and went in and poked around a bit, but had to be careful because I didn't want to fall into any of the open graves. I didn't want to break a leg and have to crawl several miles out of the woods.

There were about twenty in all, if memory serves correct, and every single one of them had a pile of dirt beside it. It was freshly dug, too, couldn't have been more than a week or so prior, I would guess. I didn't see any sign of heavy equipment, so whoever had been digging had done so by hand, so you can imagine how long it must have taken and how much work was involved, even if it was two or three people doing the digging.

The headstones were all still in place, more or less, although some of them had tumbled over while the digging was going on. I didn't see any human remains or any coffins or anything, but then again these people had been in the ground so long I figured there wasn't anything left of them anyway.

I never did figure out what happened there. I thought maybe the graves had been relocated, but for what purpose? This was miles deep into the woods and not near anything that would have required the graves to be relocated. In fact, I'm certain the old cemetery is still there to this day.

I also considered the idea of grave robbers, but again—this is way out in the middle of nowhere—the people buried out here were poor mountain folk, and I seriously doubt they would have had any valuables buried with them.

I have an inkling that it may have been in reality something more sinister, something evil, but I don't want to even think along those lines. I don't want any part of anything like that, don't even want to know about it. Anyone who would disrespect the dead like that is pure evil in my mind, pure evil.

CHAPTER 44

PHANTOM FOOTSTEPS

One time, I was out hunting along Beaver Creek, in Knox County. I had a rifle and a pistol with me, in hopes of finding a few squirrels. We didn't really know it, but we were poor back then, and any extra meat on the dinner table was a welcome blessing.

Beaver Creek runs for miles through East Tennessee and up into Virginia. The water is cold but clear and pure, and lots of animals come to it to get a drink, so it makes for good hunting. I've shot many a squirrel, raccoon and possum along its banks.

On this particular day, I had ventured farther up and along the creek than usual, up near the mouth. For some reason, I had never felt comfortable in this particular area of the creek. I always felt like I was being watched, and there were tales of large cats being spotted in the area. I myself had never seen one, but knew other folks in the area who had supposedly sighted them.

Lots of times any missing livestock or even missing pets were attributed to the mysterious cats.

I was walking along the bank, scanning the tree line, but not having much luck.

The creek was gurgling as normal, but my footsteps in the creek gravel seemed to be making more noise than usual. I knew that wasn't a good thing if I wanted to shoot any squirrels—if they heard me coming, I didn't stand a chance.

I stopped to rest for a minute, and to my surprise, it sounded like my footsteps continued. I held my breath and listened for a minute and realized I was hearing someone—or something—else walking nearby. The footsteps abruptly ceased. I stood very still and quiet for a few more minutes and, hearing nothing else, continued on.

I hadn't gone more than a few yards when I heard the other set of footsteps start up again. I would stop, and after another step or two, the others would stop as well. I scanned the area carefully, but didn't see anyone or anything else nearby. This continued for the better part of a half hour, off and on, matching my own pace.

At one point, it almost seemed that the footsteps were even with me, but coming from the other side of the creek. The creek wasn't that wide in this area, so I could see the other side plainly.

This little game went on until I reached a bend in the creek and I headed off through someone's cow pasture.

Enough was enough. I didn't want to meet up with a big cat or worse.

Like I said, I never did see or hear anything, but I did hear what sounded like something with two legs matching my pace along the creek. I wasn't scared since I had my guns with me, but they might not even have been any use since I couldn't see what was following along with me. I still venture back to that area of the creek on rare occasions, but I've never heard the footsteps again. I have no idea what it could have been.

CHAPTER 45

THE MYSTERIOUS COW PILE

This one is both funny and weird, but it happened anyway. Some friends and I were messing around in the woods, miles from anywhere, when we came upon an old barn. There had been a dairy farm in this particular place decades ago, but the river had been dammed up to make a lake, and now everything except for the barn and accompanying silo was under a dozen or more feet of water.

The barn looked like it was about ready to fall over, but being adventurous boys with more curiosity than good sense, we decided to explore it anyway.

We went inside, but there wasn't a lot to see—not much excitement in an old abandoned barn. I figured we should leave, but then one of the guys got the bright idea that we should climb up into the loft and look around.

Like I said, the barn was dead old and looked on the verge of collapse—I wasn't too keen on the idea of climbing around up in the top of it. But, ah, youth...

Rather than be called yellow or chicken, I decided to climb up with the rest of the guys.

If the barn had been boring, the loft was doubly so. Just a bunch of wobbly boards with gaps big enough to see the dirt floor some distance below. It looked like a good place to fall and break a leg or even your neck. I was getting ready to climb back down, hoping the wooden rungs would support my weight for the return trip, when one of the guys called out, "Look! Come and look at this! You won't believe it!"

The rest of us hurriedly made our way over to the corner and up to a higher side loft, where the one kid had found something exciting. It was a cow pile.

And a fresh one at that.

Now this may not seem very exciting to you. If you've ever lived on or been around a farm, you come to know cow manure as a fact of life, and you'd better watch where you step. But here, in the top loft of an ancient barn that hadn't been used in decades, was an unmistakable fresh pile of cow flop.

If you stop and think about this for a little while, you'll realize just how weird this discovery was. Number one, like I said before, the barn hadn't been in use for at least twenty or thirty years. Number two (no pun intended), even if it had still been a working farm, there would be no way for a cow to get into the upper loft on its own, nor any reason for putting one up there by manual means—the upper side loft was just a little platform under the eave of the barn, maybe twenty or thirty feet off the ground.

Yet there it was. We even poked it with a stick to ensure that, yes, it was indeed fresh. Some things are better left to the imagination, and we never could come up with a plausible reason for our discovery.

CHAPTER 46

THE VANISHED CALF

I know of a really strange encounter for which there is no explanation—at least not a rational one, anyway.

When I was just a boy, my uncle owned a small farm in the foothills of western North Carolina. Farming is a hard way to make a living, as my uncle discovered, so he used his farm to supplement the family food supply. By putting food on the table, the farm paid for itself in the long run, but they weren't solely dependent on it to survive.

The farm, although small, was diverse. They raised a huge garden in two different areas of the property, and they kept some livestock. The animals consisted of chickens for fresh eggs, and a couple of dairy cows for fresh milk and butter. I seem to recall seeing the odd pig or two and a goat from time to time as well.

Anyway, the story is that one day they had a calf go missing. Now as any small-time farmer can verify, the loss of a calf—even one, whether it be for milk or meat or sale—can be devastating.

My uncle was tasked with locating the missing calf and bringing her home. He looked high and low—yet no calf.

Think about it—I mean, how many places could a calf be? They're not that small—it's not like it could get lost or misplaced or have fallen behind something or under something, right?

But on the other hand, the woods—even on a small farm—can be a big, big place. The old 'needle in a haystack' analogy springs to mind. I guess there are lots of places a calf could get lost, after all...

Soon, darkness fell and my uncle had to abandon the hunt until first light of the next day. He had never lost a calf before, so this bothered him to a great degree. Had it been stolen? Taken by a predatory animal or animals, such as a mountain lion or a pack of wolves? Was it lying somewhere injured and in pain, or perhaps even dead? My uncle had trouble sleeping due to concern over his missing livestock.

Just as he was drifting off to sleep, around three a.m., my uncle heard a noise out in the trot between the barn and the house. He sprang up from his bed and raced out into the backyard to see if the wayward calf had returned. Much to his chagrin and dismay, he saw nothing, and the noise abruptly stopped as soon as he was halfway to the barn.

Perplexed, he stood and listened for a few minutes. He was positive he'd heard the calf lowing (which is much more subtle than bawling, that being the noise the calf would make if it were injured or in distress). Sure enough, he heard what sounded like the calf again, only this time from the other side of the house, away from the barn in the side yard.

My uncle walked over into the side yard, expecting to see the calf, only to be met with emptiness and silence. An almost eerie silence. Same as before, within a few minutes he heard the calf again. This time, it was farther back beyond the house and seemed to be coming from a hillside just above the tree line.

He slowly crept to the top of the crest, and now the noise was deeper into the trees, off to his left. Again, he followed the sound, only to have it move farther away and in a different direction every time he thought he was getting near it.

It was also about this time that he started noticing some strange lights darting among the trees at a distance. He stated that the lights were sort of glowing, almost like a fluorescent light that didn't have quite enough electricity to fully engage. Just as with the apparent sounds of the lost calf, whenever he walked close to one of the mysterious glowing lights, it would wink out silently, only to reappear a short time later, although at a considerable distance, more than a human carrying a light could travel.

By now, my uncle was developing a good case of the 'willies,' as he called it. Add in the fact that he was also no longer within sight of the house or barn, and you will begin to understand his consternation and concern. As he turned to head back toward the house before he wandered off too deep into the dark woods, he said he thought he heard voices in the distance as well, coming from the area of the lights. He further stated that one of the odd things about the voices was that (while being somewhat soft) they sounded like someone speaking the wrong speed—years later when he recounted the tale to me, he likened it to a 33 rpm phonograph record being played back at 45 rpm.

To make a long story short (and I glumly realize that we may be a bit too late in that regard), the calf was never found—not a trace. When my uncle went to the wooded hillside the next morning during the light of day, he claims to have found some odd, 'totally round' prints in the soft earth. The tracks were too small to have been left by a man-sized human, but were way too large to have been left by any kind of known animal...About eight inches across, he said, and 'as round as a pie plate.'

No blood, no hair...nor bones, nor hide—it was as if the poor calf simply ceased to be—at least in this dimension or plane of existence. While it's possible that a calf could have simply wandered off and perished, it's highly unlikely given this particular scenario.

My uncle has always been a sober and somber man, and I have no reason to doubt the description of the event as he related it to me. I heard the story a few times (usually at my insistence) both as a youth and as an adult, and the story never wavered or faltered.

My uncle stated in all honesty that he truly believes that someone (or something) abducted the calf and was using the noises to try to lure him into the woods—where he feels he would have been abducted as well.

I always keep this in the back of my mind—as a 'cautionary tale,' as it were—whenever I'm out in the woods, particularly after dark. Thank you for letting me share my uncle's strange story.

CHAPTER 47

THE DOG WHO WASN'T THERE

When I was a kid, we lived in the foothills of upstate New York. My brother, who is several years older than me, used to keep hunting dogs. He enjoyed forays into the wilderness and would occasionally hunt for raccoons or opossum. He had one particular hunting dog, a Walker coonhound named Moses, which he dearly loved. At around three years of age, Moses had become entangled in a barbed wire fence one day while my brother was at work, and the poor dog subsequently died from complications due to the injuries he suffered.

My brother took the death of his favorite coon dog pretty hard, understandably so. He had erected a nice, homemade headstone out behind my parents' barn where he'd buried his dog. The dog was a very unique-looking black, white and tan coloration, and it wouldn't have been easy to confuse him with another dog. But—a few weeks after Moses had been buried—he started showing up around our farm. Oddly enough, almost everyone in our immediate family had a paranormal encounter with the dog EXCEPT my brother.

There are many examples: One day, as my mom was hanging up the wash out by the same barn, she noticed the first sheet she'd hung was missing. A few minutes later, she saw a dog that looked exactly like Moses carrying it off into the woods and out of sight.

Another time, my dad was out working in our garden. He looked up just in time to see Moses in profile as he disappeared around the corner of our house. Intrigued, my dad dropped the hoe he was using to weed the garden and immediately took off in a trot around the same corner of the house—only to be met by absolutely no dog of any kind, let alone the phantom Moses.

I, myself, had several encounters with the ghost dog, including some in which visual contact didn't happen—I would hear a dog sniffing and whining nearby our house or barn, but would then be unable to locate any such dog. I had several visual sightings too, and it always seemed to be (like everyone else) at a particular time when Moses was rounding a corner or was just going out of sight.

Another time, my brother's wife and young son had just arrived from a shopping trip, and they spotted Moses on the edge of the woods beside the barn. My young nephew was so excited, he burst into the house exclaiming that Moses had returned. On further investigation, of course, no dog was found anywhere on our property.

We moved to the south when I was a teenager, and the ghost of the dog didn't follow us those several hundred miles. However, I do often wonder if there's not some people living on a small farm in upstate NY who often spot a ghostly hunting dog just turning the corner and then being nowhere to be found. My family was always somewhat skeptical when it came to the paranormal or supernatural, but we accepted that somehow Moses continued to stay with us even after he had passed on from this physical world.

CHAPTER 48

GHOSTLY SCHOOL BUS

[Author's Note: I don't know about you, but I find an abandoned school bus deep in the woods much more frightening than I would, say, an abandoned house...There's just something so inherently creepy about a school bus, ghostly or otherwise. This is one of my favorite stories that I collected for this volume. – Steve]

In an undisclosed area of Southern Ohio lies an abandoned stone quarry. While exploring that quarry, I had the strangest, most paranormal, most inexplicable experience of my life. I choose not to disclose the location, as I refuse to feel responsible should an irresponsible party or parties venture forth and hurt, maim or kill themselves. Caveat aside, this is my story.

When I was in grade school, I used to fancy myself a 'hunter,' and I spent many bucolic, sunlit, Kapraesque days in the woods with a Crossman BB rifle (some of you may also know this as a 'pellet gun,' as it would launch pellets as well as BBs). I had a .22 single-shot bolt-action rifle I had received as a Christmas gift, but I usually preferred the somewhat more silent BB gun when stalking prey in the woods.

I'm not proud of it now (I hung up my hunter's cap many decades ago and now campaign for animal rights), but I had a lot of patience and a good aim and racked up many slain crows in my day—at least the animals that I had chosen as targets were a bane to the farmers, so I was helping save the crops—although that seems like a thin justification now for my activities.

On one particular day, I had ridden my bicycle—Crossman rifle strapped across my back—a lot farther and in a different direction than I would usually go hunting. If you've ever been through rural Ohio, you know how one cornfield can look just like any of the other hundreds that dot any particular farming community, so anything was a welcome break to the monotony. Or so I thought, when I spotted a dry, abandoned quarry.

Oh, what luck, I thought as I secured my bike and began my descent down one of the hewn rock walls. The quarry hadn't been in use in what looked like decades, and had some good-size trees growing up from the once-submerged bottom. I was in BB-rifle, crow-hunting heaven!

I followed the edge of the steep wall and soon found myself mid-quarry, then decided to cut across the middle. Imagine my surprise when about halfway in, in a clump of blackberry briars higher than a man's head, I spied an old yellow school bus.

I say 'old' because it was of a style that harkened back to a day different than the one I currently lived in—my school bus was sleek, aerodynamic and downright modern compared to the example in front of me, which, although well worn, did not look like it had suffered years of neglect. Curious beyond belief, I picked a line and began to carefully pick my way through the briars.

After what seemed like an eternity (scratched from head to toe and oozing blood from a few dozen tiny cuts, thanks to the briars), I arrived at the bus. As luck would have it, a gentle push against the doors was all that was required to make them swing open, albeit somewhat creakily and reluctantly at first.

I entered the bus and was pleased to see that it was in good repair. All the windows were intact and closed, and the vinyl seats, although cracked with age, were present and intact. I slowly crept all the way to the back of the bus, ensuring that I had the entire vehicle to myself.

Satisfied that I was all alone, I sat down in the very last seat to rest for a bit. While relaxing, my gun laid across my lap, I even managed to wiggle the window by my seat down a crack, thinking that I could use the bus as a hunting blind and take shots at crows that might venture close for the blackberries.

While scanning the bushes for any movement, I suddenly began to hear voices approaching. Fearing I might be in trouble for being in the quarry (and aboard someone's school bus), I gently eased myself and my rifle down onto the dusty floor and tried to remain as still and as quiet as possible.

Thankfully, I had closed the doors to the bus upon my successful entry, so no one would have suspected an interloper. Sure enough, the voices grew louder still, and I could make them out clearly—it was two girls, most likely around my own age. I held my breath as I heard the doors at the front of the bus creak open. I remained still, not sure how I would explain myself when discovered.

I was relieved when I realized that the girls had chosen seats at the front of the bus. I peered under the seats and could see their feet beneath the seat where they had perched. They were speaking in quiet, hushed (almost conspiratorial) tones, so I really couldn't make out what was being discussed. After a few minutes, I watched as one girl exited the bus.

I risked discovery and peeked over the top of the seats, observing a dark-haired girl wearing a stocking cap still sitting in the seat. In a few moments, I heard footsteps and observed the other girl, with longer blond hair and also wearing a stocking cap, climb back into the bus. In her hands was some sort of serving tray (looking back, I think it may have been a school lunch tray) containing two mugs. The blond girl placed the tray on the adjacent seat, closed the bus doors, and then served whatever was in the mugs. It was cold enough that I could see my breath, but I don't recall seeing any steam rising from the cups—or from the girls' breath either, for that matter.

I decided it looked like I was going to be here awhile, so I slid back under my seat in the back and proceeded to wait them out. After about twenty to thirty minutes, I noticed it had grown completely still and quiet in the bus. I no longer heard the frantic whisperings or the sounds of shifting in the seats. Carefully, I eased my head up for another peek—only to discover that I was completely alone in the school bus.

At first I thought maybe I was mistaken, and assumed that maybe the girls had done the same thing I had and were resting either across the seats or even on the floor. I left my rifle in the back of the bus, so as not to frighten them with it, and walked stealthily to the front of the bus. No one was there.

Perplexed, I returned to the back of the bus and retrieved my BB gun. It was starting to get dark, and I didn't want to be caught out in an unfamiliar area after dark—trying to climb the rough rocks out of the quarry in the dark probably wouldn't have been a good idea.

The bus doors were closed, and I even tried opening and closing them a few times. No matter how fast or slow or rough or gentle I worked the doors, they still made a distinctive sound. There was no way they could have left via the doors without my having heard them.

I'm not sure exactly what I witnessed that day, but I'm sure it was of paranormal or supernatural origin. I didn't revisit the quarry until later in the winter when I returned with a friend. I had told him all about my mysterious encounter with the bus and the girls. He eyed me suspiciously when we arrived in the middle of the quarry—and found nothing but a huge patch of berry briars. There was no evidence that a bus had ever been inside the briar patch.

I now feel that this was something meant for me to experience. I have yet to fully understand the meaning, but it was essentially a turning point in my life, and I can trace back to that moment when I began to realize the 'gift' that I have, and I have spent the rest of my life learning how to use it to help others.

CHAPTER 49

JOANNA'S CABIN

When I was a kid, I used to go with my parents to visit my cousin Joanna, who owned a cabin in Townsend, Tennessee. Townsend is known as 'the quiet side of the Smokies,' a world removed from the not-so-quiet side of the Great Smoky Mountains, the uber-touristy Gatlinburg and total mondo tourist trap of Pigeon Forge.

Joanna and her husband, William, actually lived in nearby Knoxville, where they were both schoolteachers. The cabin, deep in the woods, was their sanctuary away from the city and screaming, rowdy elementary school students. We most often visited in the fall, when the Smokies were awash in color with their world-famous foliage.

I'm guessing that the cabin was built during the early part of the twentieth century, best guess between 1920 and 1930. And as such, and this was in the 1970s, there were at least five decades during which someone could have died and returned to haunt the cabin.

Not only the cabin, but the whole area of woods surrounding it felt strange—it just felt 'off,' if you know what I mean…You folks who investigate haunted locations will know exactly the kind of feeling I'm describing. It's a very real, very palpable feeling, very high emotion.

The most activity inside the cabin seemed to take place in the room at the very back of the dwelling. It was an unused bedroom when I was a kid, and I was usually relegated to this area to play quietly so as not to disturb the grown-ups while they chatted over coffee—like I said, both my cousin and her husband were lifelong elementary schoolteachers, so the last thing they wanted while trying to relax was some little hellion like myself running around and making noise.

So I would sit in the back room and read a book, sometimes for hours. On the first occasion that I had a paranormal experience, I had walked into the back room and sat down on the floor and was minding my own business with a book. All of a sudden, a rocking chair on the other side of the room started rocking slowly, as if someone unseen was sitting in it and relaxing. The rocking chair was near a window, so I would have easily spotted any string or fishing line or anything that would have indicated hijinks on the part on any of the adults—plus the chance that any of them would have even tried to scare me would have been at least a billion to one. It was much more preferable to them that I remain silent and out of sight.

I tore into the living room where the adults were, blubbering at the top of my lungs about a ghost in the back bedroom. The adults more or less dismissed me, my cousin and her husband in particular. I suppose the only thing worse than a know-it-all kid is a couple of smug, know-it-all schoolteachers!

They tried as they might to tell me that nothing had happened, but I know what I saw—it's just as clear in my mind to this day as any other memory from the same time period. That cabin is haunted as all get-out! That was my last trip to the cabin, and that's been over ten years ago now—I will never go back there if it can be helped—no thanks!

CHAPTER 50

SCRATCHING AT THE TENT

Some friends from school and I had a strange experience years ago in the Great Smoky Mountains National Park. We were camping in one of the designated areas near Clingman's Dome. In the middle of the night, we heard something large lumbering through the mountain forest. Whatever it was, it came right up to our tent and was scratching like it was trying to get in.

My friend Paul actually ended up cutting the back of the tent with his camp knife, and we dove out the back and ran off down the trail in the dark—probably not the smartest move that could have been made, but we were scared out of our wits. Looking back, I think, *What if one of us had gotten hurt?* For example, Paul was a rather large fellow (six feet one and easily 250 lbs), and there's no way my skinny self and the other friend camping with us (he was skinny, too) could have carried him back down the mountain. When it was discussed later on, Paul mused we would have just had to leave him to be eaten (or whatever fate awaited) if he'd broken a leg or ankle that night.

Comparing memories later on, we all agreed that at the time we could make out a large hulking shape that was wreaking havoc on our campsite. The black bears that are indigenous to the Smokies can get fairly large, but this thing would have made two or three black bears. We've all hesitated to say it for fear of ridicule, but we are fairly certain it was a Bigfoot or similar creature.

That night, we ran off down the trail and slept in our car. The next morning, we warily crept back to our former campsite, grabbed up as much as we could carry, and fled. I guess it kind of goes without saying that we never went camping in that particular area again. I've been all over the area many times since, but always in daylight. To me, there's just been too many strange disappearances over the years in the Smokies to take any chances after dark.

CHAPTER 51

THE PHANTOM WOODSMAN

I had an argument with my then boss and decided to go out for a walk in the woods to cool off. And by a 'walk in the woods,' I intended for it to be just that—a walk—not a hike or an excursion or a journey—and certainly not an ordeal that could have cost me my life.

The area in which I decided to go for a walk was part of a state park, so I thought stomping through the woods would be better than stomping on my boss's head and thus ending my perfectly clean record—I had never been arrested or even suspected of anything, so I was kind of already unnerved that I had let Keith (my boss at the time) get under my skin so bad with mere words. Looking back, I think he meant well and was trying to push me into giving my best—but as a then nineteen-year-old, I knew better and was insulted rather than taking his pep talk to heart. I've never been a violent person, have never hit anyone in anger, so this was one of my secrets. My relief mechanism was walking it off in the forests of Ohio.

On this particular day, I wasn't paying too much attention to where I was going once I arrived at the state park. I parked my truck and locked it up in the parking area, strapped on a small daypack and my Garmin GPS, and stomped off into the woods and solace, at long last.

Let me stop right here to say that I learned a valuable lesson that day. First of all, if you're going into the woods, even for fifteen minutes, pack enough supplies (i.e., food, water, matches, candles, a change of clothes, dry socks, etc.) as if you were going into the woods for a minimum of two days...Literally, this one simple act of overpreparing could save your life.

And, oh yes, batteries. By all means pack batteries. Especially if you have things you depend on that need them—like a flashlight. And (argh) a Garmin GPS that can lead you back to the parking lot, even in total, absolute darkness. Yes, the batteries in my GPS died, by my estimation, about two hours into the trip. And if you've ever been in deep woods—well away from the ambient light and light pollution of the city—you realize the kind of total, absolute darkness I'm describing being lost within.

So here I was, gathering my thoughts and getting all calm and collected in the middle of the woods. Ahh, glorious nature. Now, about the time I calmed down and was once again at peace with myself, I had a few sudden revelations dawn upon me...

Revelation number one: It is dark.

Revelation number two: It is getting cold.

Revelation number three: I have no idea where I am located, other than in a state park.

Revelation number four immediately followed when I whipped out my trusty Garmin GPS, only to watch it chuckle weakly then die completely when I tried to power it on.

As you may have guessed, none of these myriad of Revelations could be considered A Good Thing at the time. Nay, in fact, rest assured that they were all Very, Very Bad Things.

My first thought (that wasn't filled with expletives) was to get a look at the night sky and see if I could chart a course by the stars. As luck would have it, I was in a low valley (what they call a 'holler' down South) and couldn't see the night sky due to the centuries of tree cover above my head, provided by the old-growth timber. Furthermore, even if I had been on the highest point in the park and standing on my tiptoes, I still wouldn't have been able to see the first celestial body with which to guide myself—the sky was completely overcast. And a light rain was beginning to fall. Lovely.

So now I really was in a pickle. Lost, in the dark, without food, water, a change of clothes or batteries for my GPS, in the cold and rain. And I had also neglected to tell nary a soul where I was going or when I should be expected back. Brilliant, simply brilliant.

It was the beginning of my 'weekend' too—I was off from work and away from the devil (aka my boss) for the next two entire days—meaning it would be more than forty-eight hours (more like sixty) before I would even be missed at work. Sigh.

I did what anyone would do in the circumstances (in fact, it really is what most people do, and they don't even realize it—I didn't)...I started walking in circles.

Now, that's not to say I thought about it and decided, *Gee, you know what, I bet if I started walking in circles, everything will be cool and groovy.* No, I was actually trying to walk back to the parking lot and my truck. I kept thinking something would look familiar and I would find the way back. But after a couple of frustrating hours of passing what appeared to be the same rocks and trees (they were), I admitted that since I was lost, I was probably walking in circles (I was). So essentially, I wasted two hours of energy for nothing, only making myself more tired, more wet and more cold in the process. So I decided to do the next thing that most people do in these types of situations: I sat down by a tree and cried. Really, I did.

After regaining my composure from the sobbing, I decided the third best thing to do would be to try to find some kind of shelter, out of the increasingly heavy rain. Of course, the best time to pick out a spot to shelter is in the daytime and plan ahead for when you need it—not after it's dark and cold and rainy and you're already wet and lost. Oh, and hungry...I forgot to mention that...By this time I was starving.

I slept a little—a fitful, miserable sleep. Looking back, I seriously doubt I slept more than an hour or two. I had been up most of the night, and when I dozed and awakened, I could just make out the faintest glimmer of dawn beginning to subtly peek over the far mountainside.

I groaned as I stood, having spent the night on the cold, damp ground had definitely taken its toll on my joints. At least I hadn't succumbed to hypothermia—at least not yet—so I at least had that to be (somewhat) thankful for, I suppose...

The rain was still falling, although it was just more of a damp misting variety rather than a soaking downpour. I guess at the time I was counting my blessings that the drops were almost microscopic, but I was still soaked to the skin either way. Oddly enough, I felt kind of warm inside my damp clothes, I suppose it was because my body was losing heat faster than normal. This thought scared me—I didn't want to die—not now, not out here in these desolate woods...

On the second day, now in progress, I became convinced that I was going to die. I had already resolved myself to accept this fate. I was going to die out here, alone, deep in the woods. I'd never see my family or friends again, and the next time they saw me—if they ever did—I'd be a skeleton in some rotting clothes. And that's if the animals of the forest didn't gnaw and scatter my bones.

A couple of times, I actually sat or lay down at the base of a tree, thinking this looks like a nice, comfortable place to draw my last breath. But over time, sometimes without even realizing it, I would get up and start walking again.

As I trudged along, I started hearing what I thought was my heart pounding in my ears, except that it sounded too slow for my heart. *Great*, I thought, *my heart will just stop, and I'll roll down the mountain into a gully and become squirrel food.* I was exhausted to the point that I was, without realizing it, basically delirious and on the verge of having visual and aural hallucinations.

Then it slowly dawned on me (my brain was working in slow motion) that the rhythmic *thud, thud, thud* I was hearing wasn't my heartbeat at all, but rather someone chopping wood. Okay, cool. There was a lumberjack or a woodsman about.

Wait! Another person! I was saved! Suddenly, after what seemed like I had been sleepwalking for hours and hours, I was wide awake and almost running toward the sound of the woodsman's axe.

Sure enough, I soon saw a guy in red and black flannel flailing away slowly and methodically at a tree with a double-bladed axe. I staggered up to him and blurted out my predicament. I vaguely remember him apologizing for not having any food or water to offer me, or any dry clothes, but he could show me the way out. He just kind of pointed up a steep bank off to my left. I thanked him and began working my way up the steep embankment by grabbing small saplings and hoisting myself up the hundred or so feet to the top.

After what seemed like forever, I finally made the top and collapsed on the edge of a packed dirt road. I had been close all along, but still had no idea which way to go. Exhausted, I was content to just sit for a while. Shortly I heard the sound of an approaching vehicle. As luck would have it, a park service truck appeared momentarily, and I waved the ranger down. I wasn't going to die out here after all.

I imagine I looked like an insane person, and the ranger kind of eyed me unbelievingly when I told him about the woodcutter just down the slope. He told me to get in and help myself to a bottle of water and some packs of peanut butter snack crackers lying on the seat. I only had to be invited once, as it all tasted like pure heaven to me.

The ranger disappeared over the side of the road and reappeared a few minutes later. When I asked about the woodcutter, he only muttered something about us being at the park service station in a few minutes. When we got there, he and the other ranger decided it would be best if they called an ambulance from the county and had me go to the hospital to be looked over —I'm sure I looked a fright.

Before the ambulance came, I once again asked the ranger about the guy cutting wood—I hoped I hadn't gotten him in any trouble. The ranger looked me straight in the eye and said, "Son, there wasn't anyone down there. No sign anyone had been there recently, and certainly no one cutting trees down. We sort of frown on that sort of thing."

He patted me on the shoulder and that was the end of the discussion, so I just let it go at that.

Looking back, I realize that I probably was near death, and I may have been hallucinating. But the man with the axe whom I saw and talked to was as real as you or me. I can't explain it other than to say there are some things that can't be explained.

CHAPTER 52

MACABRE MUSEUM

I came across the remains of an old shack out in the middle of the woods. It looked like it was ready to fall over, and the roof sagged heavily in places. I found the door ajar and went inside, curious to see what type of detritus might have been left behind from the previous occupants. What I found chilled me to the bone.

Set on crude shelves, there was a prominent display of bones, weird carvings and strange-looking stones with what appeared to be runes carved into them. There were things in liquid in jars, some sort of specimens, I suppose?

There were also bizarre lines of words—possibly dark poetry of some fashion—written in inch-high black boxcar letters all around the room. I managed to locate the stub of an almost used-up wax candle and lit it with my cigarette lighter.

Above the door, I saw the words "A curse be upon you," which kind of freaked me out—if you were going to threaten me with a curse, shouldn't it be on the outside of the shack?

I'm not sure just who set up this macabre museum out in the woods (or, more importantly, why), but it may be one of those cases where it's better not to know—if you catch my drift. Kids having a laugh? Heavy metal dude bros recreating their favorite album cover? Hardcore Satanists deep in the woods? Your guess is as good as mine...

CHAPTER 53

DEMON FROG

I found something really strange out in the woods once. Let me tell you about it. I was in this area hunting. It was on a farm, and I'm not going to name any names, but I did have permission to be on the land.

Now this old farmer, from what I'd heard, would allow anyone permission to be on his land, but you had to ask. Well, what I heard was that there were some witches who had asked to use his land, and he had said okay to them. Now, depending on what you hear and who you ask, some folks say they were witches and some folks say they were devil worshippers.

Me, I know the difference. My grandma was from what they always called the Old Country, and she was a witch. A gypsy witch. She told fortunes and whatnot, made love spells for teenage girls to cast to get themselves a boyfriend, and stuff like that...That ain't no devil worship—that's just being a witch!

Now, back to what I was saying—so anyway, this old farmer had given me permission to hunt squirrel on his land. I had gone out there one day about five o'clock in the evening after school and I was looking around. I had my rifle with me, as always—back then you could walk around with a rifle and no one thought twice about it. It was just a .22, nothing scary about it.

I hadn't really thought I'd get much of anything squirrel wise that day, it was more of just a scouting trip. It was really too late in the day to do any serious hunting. You want to hunt squirrel, you got to get up early, already be in the woods when daylight breaks. Squirrels are early risers, so you have to rise even earlier than they do!

Here I was, just moseying along, looking for squirrel nests up in the trees, any signs that might show me where to come back, when I saw someone moving through the woods out of the corner of my eye. My senses were sharp back then, and there wasn't much I didn't notice, especially in the woods.

I slid behind a tree and squatted down, doing my best not to be noticed and see what this other person was up to out here in these deep woods. Whoever it was must have come up from the creek, because no one had passed me, and I hadn't passed anyone on the little game trail that wound through the forest. The growth was too dense otherwise, and if you'd tried to come straight through the woods, you would have made more noise than a boar in a briar patch.

When the person got a little closer and drew up almost even with me, I could see that it was a woman, actually a girl, maybe eighteen, nineteen years old—she was young, but a little bit older than I was. She was wearing all black and had long dark hair. Now, I ain't afraid of stuff, and I don't pay no never mind to all them spooky tales folks like to swap, but she did give me a creepy feeling, just the way she looked and because I certainly hadn't been expecting to see such a sight out here in the woods.

I maneuvered around so that I could see better, but still held my secret position and didn't let her know I was there by making any noise. She hadn't spotted me, as far as I could tell. She laid a burlap bundle down in the dirt and began carefully unwrapping it. I couldn't see what it was, but she took something out of the bundle and set it up in the hollowed-out place in the crotch of a knotty, gnarled-looking tree.

She lit some little candle stubs and said some words I couldn't make out—she might have even been speaking in some witch language, I reckon. I'm sure my eyes was as big as saucers, because I ain't never seen nothing like this before or since. Satisfied with whatever she'd done, the girl put out the candle stubs and lit off back through the woods the way she'd come. Of course now I was a mite curious, so I waited a little spell to make sure she wasn't going to double back. When I was sure she wasn't, I slowly crept over to the hollow tree and had a look inside. Imagine my surprise when I saw a grinning demon frog looking back at me!

I jumped back, and to be honest, it took all the courage I could muster not to holler out loud—that thing was that scary! I slowly peeked in again, prepared this time. The frog I could see now wasn't real, but seemed to be made out of rubber. I really didn't want to touch it, but I did give it a poke with the tip of my finger, and it jiggled a little. It was like a frog in a sitting position like a human, and it had human facial features and some kind of weird, pointy ears. I reckon it was a frog—I ain't never seen nothing like it in real life though!

I'd had enough spooks for one night, so I cut a fast walk back to the house. I heard other folks talk about the weird stuff that goes on back there in the woods, and I believe it—because I'm a witness to it!

CHAPTER 54

CUMBERLAND FALLS GHOSTS

Cumberland Falls is located in Kentucky, not far from Monticello. It's close to DuPont Lodge, which was once a destination for the wealthy elite of the robber barons of the early twentieth century. The falls are famous for the 'moonbow,' which is a rainbow visible in the dark. There is only one other place, Victoria Falls in South Africa, where this phenomenon occurs. Apparitions, spook lights and more have been spotted in the heavily wooded areas away from the tourist areas of both the park and lodge.

There are a couple of different legends about the 'White Lady of the Falls,' a bride who either slipped over the falls accidentally and drowned or was murdered by a jealous rival suitor of her husband-to-be. Either way, whichever story you hear, the end result is the same—a woman died in the water at Cumberland Falls, and her ghost can be spotted around the base of the falls at night. Additionally, a lot of people have gone over the falls over the past few decades (some by accident and, sadly, some on purpose), and it's said that all these spirits haunt the area below the falls as well.

Up above the falls, there also used to be a hotel that burned down and a ferry that capsized, killing many people. It's not unusual to hear moans and cries coming from the woods on the far side of the falls on dark nights. I've spent a lot of time hanging out around the falls at night, and there is a certain heaviness, a certain creepiness in the air—if you've ever been to extremely haunted locations, such as the battlefield at Gettysburg, then you know exactly the type of feeling I'm trying to describe.

As well, the area immediately down below the falls is haunted. Just behind the falls is a cavern—not a lot of people know this—and the park tries to keep it a secret. I'm not advocating anything illegal, of course, but I will say that anyone who is determined enough can get inside the cool cavern. There have been reports of ghostly sounds and voices from decades past being heard to echo throughout the cave. Once, I had gone hoping to see the moonbow. However, as conditions have to be so perfect, on occasion there would be no moonbow. Instead, I spent the hours from midnight until about 3 a.m. exploring the caves under the falls. I never saw anyone, but at one point I heard someone way, way back in the cavern singing an old hymn. I decided it was time for me to go after that.

Aside from the park and designated areas, there are a lot of 'forgotten' areas in the woods nearby, holdovers from the good old days. Staircases that lead nowhere, crumbling foundations, lone chimneys. In short, it's a very spooky and spectacular area to go to after dark.

CHAPTER 55

BALL LIGHTNING

Ball lightning is a natural phenomenon, but that doesn't make it any less frightening. I had the distinct pleasure of witnessing ball lightning in the forest during an epic thunderstorm several years ago.

It didn't really even look like rain when I left to go on a joy hike, but did it ever blow up an electrical storm. I was able to seek shelter under the overhang of a rock outcropping for the worst of the storm, but I still ended up soaked to the skin—it was one of the tremendous storms, full of boom-bang thunder and lightning and the wind pelting the rain as it blew it sideways. Quite the spectacle!

From my vantage point inside the tiny, cavelike hidey-hole, I watched as rain beat down with a fury. In addition to what appeared to be silver-dollar-sized raindrops, hail between the size of a dime and a quarter also began to bounce off the forest floor. Thankfully, I was only soaked to the skin, but at least I wasn't having chunks of ice bounced off my head!

Suddenly, there was a blinding flash of light with a thunderous boom on top. You know how you can tell the distance of a storm by counting the seconds between the flash of lightning and the resultant boom? Well, these were instantaneous—you would have needed scientific instruments to calculate what must have been a few scant milliseconds!

The forest immediately took on a 'heaviness' that I don't think I can accurately describe. The very air was damp, and the familiar smell of ozone permeated the area. Off to my left, I heard what I'll call a sizzling noise, and I turned to face it.

Although it was daylight, it was dark inside the forest, in part due to the heavy foliage and also in part due to angry black storm clouds that filled the sky horizon to horizon. I observed what I first thought to be someone approaching with a very bright searchlight. On closer inspection, it was an orb of extremely bright light, and it was 'bouncing' down the dirt path that led through the woods.

Mystified, I'm sure my mouth was hanging open as I watched the ball bounce and seemingly roll past. The sizzle was louder now, and there was also a subtone, a low electronic buzz, kind of like you hear near high-tension power lines.

The ball of light, which now was very close and seemed as bright as the sun, rolled past me on down the path and bounced into a tree, hitting the trunk solidly about three feet above the forest floor. There was a loud "bang!" and an even brighter flash, like a giant flashbulb going off, and then nothing...The ball lightning was gone.

There was still a heavy smell of ozone in the air—the air practically still tingled with electricity—I'm guessing the charge that the ball lightning dispersed was still hanging in the damp air particles. Soon, the storm passed over the valley I was in, and headed over the other side of the ridge. When it let up enough, I headed home and made it without further incident. I consider myself fortunate to have witnessed such a spectacular natural phenomenon as ball lightning—and to have lived to tell about it!

CHAPTER 56

SURF'S UP

The weirdest, most unexplainable thing that ever happened to me was up near Cumberland Gap [Tennessee] back in the late 1960s. I was just a kid, maybe ten or eleven years old, and we didn't live too far from the Gap. Nowadays, they'd probably put you in jail for it (or at least call the sheriff on you), but back then I used to go hunting in the woods with my BB gun—it was something all the boys did until they were old enough to hunt with a real rifle. I admit, I did shoot a bird or two, but usually the only thing I caught was a stiff neck from walking around in the woods looking up!

This time, it was quiet in the woods. I figured something had the birds scared into being quiet. If a snake or bobcat or other predator (even another human) was around, the birds would stay quiet. So something had the birds spooked. I kept walking around looking up, but they were all hid out.

About that time, I walked into a clearing, and when I did, I caught sight of something way, way up in the sky. It was a bright, clear day, and at first I thought I was seeing a small plane —maybe like a Piper Cub or something similar.

As I continued watching, it soon became evident that the object was falling, and tumbling as it fell. As it got closer, I then decided maybe it was a glider plane since it was silent. As it grew closer still, I was finally able to see that it was much too small to be an airplane or a glider. Maybe a remote-control hobby plane? I thought. That would be cool to find one of those!

As the object drew nearer, now just above the treetops, I could see it spinning lazily in the sun. I could at long last see that it wasn't a remote-control plane, either, but what looked like a plane's wing. I felt a chill as I realized I may be looking at floating wreckage from a plane crash!

I ran down the hill through the woods to approximately where I noticed the object was headed. I thought if it was part of a plane wing that had come off in flight, I'd probably get my picture in the paper with it if I retrieved it.

Sure enough, I hadn't much more than lost sight of it through the leaf canopy, when I heard something crashing through the trees over to my left. As I ran over, I watched the object strike the ground, bounce end over end, then come to a final stop with a small thud. I raced over, heart pounding, only to discover—a surfboard?

What the heck? Seriously, it was a surfboard, and a nice one at that. It was the kind that is fiberglass laminate over a Styrofoam core. The fiberglass was somewhat scratched up, probably from falling through the trees. There was also a 'bite-shaped' chunk missing near the nose of the board—I figured this had happened as it plummeted through the tall trees as well.

Imagine my folks' surprise when I came home from hunting, having bagged a surfboard instead of a bird! I kept the board for years, occasionally taking it to the lake near my house just to paddle around on. I left it in the crawlspace when my parents and I moved out of my childhood home in the late '70s, I'm guessing it was around 1978 or 1979.

How did the board get in the sky? I doubt it fell out of an airplane, as I would have seen and or at least heard one going by prior. Apparently, there was a big storm over the coast of the Outer Banks of North Carolina around that time—but keep in mind that I was in Tennessee, right on the Kentucky border, and easily a few hundred miles inland from the coast. How did this happen? Your guess is as good as mine.

CHAPTER 57

STRANGE MACHINES

[Author's Note: This story is very similar to another included in this book, titled 'Mysterious Sphere.' While both stories are from Oak Ridge, Tennessee, and about the same time period, I decided to include both. The persons who told me the original stories did not know each other, yet had almost the same type of experience, which I feel makes these all the more fascinating. – Steve]

What were those strange machines we witnessed in the woods as kids? I'm thinking it was some sort of government/military doings, or maybe even a 'mad scientist/inventor' situation.

Some of the machines appeared to march across the field, autonomous, while others—perhaps if only for their sheer size and complexity—simply must have had a human operator inside.

Keep in mind that the area where my friends and I grew up

as children was very heavily vested in the military-industrial complex. In fact, there for a decade or so in the 1960s, Oak Ridge had more PhDs per capita than any other city in the world.

So, you take that mix—nuclear physicists, rocket heads, gearheads, robotics dreamers, and basically scientists of every tool and die and flavor and discipline—and it would have been more stunning to me in retrospect if we didn't have some nut running around in the suburbs, building potentially harmful machines.

We'd take our fishing poles and head to the lake—the beautiful Melton Hill, a result of the Tennessee Valley Authority's damming of the Clinch River—and set off into those dewy, bucolic summer morns of decades past. Days like those only exist now in the hearts and minds of those lucky enough to have experienced them the first go-round. Simply put, I don't think days like that—perfect days, with the optimal temperature, warm glowing light, and cool, refreshing, delicious breezes— exist anymore. Like boyhood, days of that caliber have vanished into the mists of time itself.

Some days, we wouldn't see the fantastical machines at all. Just quiet sounds of nature and the gentle rhythm of the lake water lapping against the shore. Other times, there would be what seemed like at least half a dozen of the infernal machines out amongst the tall grass on the other side of the lake.

We had entertained the idea of 'borrowing' one of our neighbors' aluminum boats and seeing how close we could get. But, alas, opportunities missed and all that—the land was government controlled, a part of the Oak Ridge Reservation, and the US Atomic Energy Commission (as well as the Department of Energy, later on) took a dim view of anyone waltzing onto their land and seeing what they were doing, much less some nosy-parker grade-school lads who were easily excitable and still proverbially wet behind the ears.

Or it may have been on the Tennessee Valley Authority's easement rather than that of the Atomic Energy Commission. Or even private land, belonging to some demented farmer with a shotgun full of buckshot and a vicious dog that loved to chomp the rear ends of little boys who were too curious and best keep to fishing.

Either way, whoever—or whatever—controlled those fascinating machines was never known. We simply chose to admire them from afar, from our hidden perches and secret tree forts from the safe distance that having a body of water between you and whatever you're watching provides.

One thing that immediately springs to mind, none of the machines were shiny or new looking. Not a single, solitary one. They were muted, rust-colored beasts, or perhaps the dull clay-red and nonreflective gray of automobile body primer.

No glints from the sun, no reflections from windows or port-holes. If not for the undeniable movement, we might not ever have noticed them at all, moving silently, doing whatever bidding for which they had been secretly constructed.

Now, Oak Ridge is home to some high-tech manufacturing companies, such as RemoTec, which specialize in robotics, in particular those sent into hazardous situations. The forerunner, the spirit, of a tech company like this may well have been founded by a lone inventor away from prying eyes.

I suppose it'll have to remain a mystery. I have even considered that the real reasons behind the weird machines we observed is truly more stale and benign than those we conjured up in our fertile, young imaginations. But it sure is enjoyable to look backward upon those halcyon days (as trite as that sounds) of living in 'The Atomic City' of Oak Ridge in the early 1970s, and not really finding 'killer robots' running amok in the fields to be that far out of the ordinary. Now that is a special childhood, indeed.

CHAPTER 58

THE MAN IN THE SWAMP

I was working as a night watchman out at the low-level radiation disposal incinerator out on Bear Creek Road in East Tennessee. One night while making my rounds, I saw a man in old-timey clothes standing in a swampy area out beside one of the buildings.

The area in question was heavily fenced off—there was no way a person could have easily gotten in, as there were two separate chain-link fences with barbed wire as well as razor wire running around the top. Plus, just for good measure and to add potential injury to insult, the water in the swampy area was 'hot,' meaning there was the distinct possibility of active radioactive runoff in it.

I called out to the man, trying to get his attention so that I could tell him to get the heck out of the swamp, if he knew what was good for him. He didn't seem to be paying any attention to me, as I continued to yell and gesticulate wildly.

This little bit of pantomime went on for a few minutes

before the man finally turned around. He made eye contact, smiled an economical smile...and then faded away, like so much smoke or fog beginning to dissipate. I was in a cold sweat, but managed to find my senses after a few moments and then wandered back inside.

I finished out my shift and left in the daylight, never to return. Looking back, I've tried to convince myself that I was tired or somehow delirious and imagined the whole ordeal. However, I know that the incident really did happen the way I described it above.

CHAPTER 59

HAT MAN

When I was a little girl back in the 1960s, we used to go and visit my grandmama and my aunties in the little town of Dunn, North Carolina. They were all originally from Louisiana, but one too many floods in the Delta had finally displaced them from their ancestral home.

Dunn is an odd town to begin with. In the past, there have been a lot of unexplainable happenings in this small town. From monsters to ghosts to the 'cavortings of a little man the size of a Coke bottle,' Dunn has more or less something weird for everyone.

I was all of six years old, and it was the first time I remember seeing my grandmama and my aunties. They had come to stay with Mama for a while after I was born, but of course I don't remember anything about that. They lived in an old house, I'm guessing from the Victorian era, on the outskirts of town.

Our visit was during the summertime, and I was outside at just about twilight, marveling at being able to chase lightning bugs—we didn't have those in the city where I lived with Mama and Daddy. I got a little braver and a little braver, despite the growing dark, and before I realized what had happened, I had wandered off quite a ways from the safety of Grandmama and the aunties' front porch with the comforting glow of the yellow porch light.

I was at the edge of some deep woods when I suddenly spotted a man standing off to one side, partially obscured by shadows, yet watching me very intently. He was dressed in all black and was wearing an odd-looking stovepipe-style tall hat and smoking a pipe.

I knew better than to talk to strangers, so I didn't say anything, but I couldn't help but stare at the man. It didn't seem to bother him any, being stared at, and he stared at me in return. After what seemed like hours (but I'm sure it was just a few minutes), his dark face broke into a huge, broad grin and I saw his face illuminated in the glow from the pipe he was puffing— and his eyes were as black as coal!

Now, I was scared silly and broke in a dead run back toward Grandmama's. When I hit the porch, I was screaming and crying to beat the band. Grandmama must have heard me coming (unless she was stone deaf, I don't see how she could have kept from hearing!) and met me at the screen door. My mama and daddy had gone down to the drive-in to get us all some dinner, so it was just Grandmama and the aunties in the house. Within a few minutes, I had a rapt audience.

After they got me calmed down to where I could talk and had blown my nose a few times, I related my tale of the dark man who'd smiled at me, the one with the tall hat and the pipe and the eyes as black as coal.

"Guede," my grandmama said with authority. My aunties nodded their heads in silent agreement. Now to my knowledge, neither my grandmama nor her spinster sisters ever practiced any form of voodoo. However, having grown up in rural Louisiana, I'm sure they knew some practitioners of this old African religion. It wasn't until I was almost grown that I found out exactly who 'Guede' is—he's one of the spirits summoned forth during a voodoo ritual and has to be appeased lest you incur his vengeance.

My grandmama and the aunties placed an offering in a plate outside on the porch, and as far as I know, it worked like a charm, as I haven't had an encounter with Guede since!

CHAPTER 60

A HAUNTED SCHOOL

When I was a teenager growing up in California, some friends and I used to go hang out and party at the remains of an old abandoned school, which had been gutted by fire. I'm not sure how many were killed, but the story I always heard repeated was that a bunch of kids and at least one teacher died.

The roof and the insides were completely gone; the only thing still standing was the walls. It had burned quite a while ago, like years and years—in fact, there were rather large trees growing inside the walls where the floor had once been. We used to go up there a lot when I was in high school, and there were always groups of people up there, mostly other kids from our school or other high schools in the area. It was almost like a local rite of passage...you had to make at least one trip to the haunted school to prove your mettle.

It may have been due to the drug use in the area—I'm convinced that certain drug activities open 'doorways' if you will—doorways that should otherwise remain firmly closed. LSD, DMT, peyote—basically anything mind-altering can cause similar circumstances, and the energy collected from the drug-fueled participants can often 'gather' in a place, for lack of a better phrase, and interact with non-drug users, if that makes sense.

One night, several of us were sitting around inside the walls. Granted, looking back, this was probably far from the safest thing we could have done. I didn't think at the time how easy it would be for those walls to collapse. I guess the truly safest thing to do would have been to stay at home!

Anyway, we were sitting 'inside' the school in the dark. I think there were about ten of us, including two or three girls who had never been up there before and were, of course, scared out of their minds. There was beer and pot and acid too. We were partying it up in this creepy place. All of a sudden the trees—some sort of pines, if I recall correctly—all bent over from the top down, the tips almost reaching the ground. It scared the crap out of us, and we all ran out. I know people will say it was the booze and drugs, but the thing is EVERYONE saw it happen, including the new girls, who were not drinking or high in the least.

Other times, always when we were sitting in complete darkness, we would hear what sounded like little kids laughing and playing. Normally, that's not a creepy sound—but out in the dark woods, in an allegedly haunted, burned-out school at three o'clock in the morning—it's frightening beyond belief. No matter how brave, or full of bravado or booze or drugs, people would scatter like scared little rabbits when the incidents would occur.

I moved away from the area in the '90s and have never been back, not even to visit friends or family who are still in the area.

I last heard that the walls finally did collapse, and the haunted school is just a pile of overgrown bricks now. But I still dare you to go back in those woods at night and not experience something supernatural!

CHAPTER 61

THE MAN IN THE TREE

I had a strange thing happen to me in the woods once, when I was a teenager spending the summer in Ohio. My mother had inherited a dairy farm near Centerville from her parents when they passed away. The farm was no longer a working farm and hadn't been for several decades. As such, it was creepy and spooky to me, even though I was a brooding young lass of thirteen years old and was fearless for the most part.

There's just something about a place that was once lively and full of life, that when it shuts down and goes into disrepair, there's a sadness—a pathos, if you will—that begins to be associated with it. It's like you can see the life and the light draining slowly out of the barns and buildings. Even the trees looked sad and forlorn.

So I was out being all Goth—full of dejection and despair and enjoying feeling lonely (I was kind of a strange teenager), wandering the woods in our new old family farm...Not the most gothic thing in the world, I reckon, but when you're an angst-ridden teenager in the middle of the Ohio heartland, you do the best you can with what you have...

I was probably about a half a mile or so out in the woods, far enough that I could no longer see the farmhouse, so it felt very alone. I had a notebook with me, which I always carried at the time. It was full of my drawings and dark poetry and that kind of stuff. Like I said, I was a very strange teenager. I came across the most magical-looking little clearing in the woods—it almost looked like the fairy circles in England that I had seen pictures of in some of my magazines. I immediately decided this would be an excellent little spot to do 'theater in the round' and put on a little poetry show, consisting of me and my dark verses being read aloud, in a dramatic performance style.

I let it all out. The little clearing was just what I needed, and I let loose wave after wave of Goth angst and sadness. I'm sure I gave what would have been considered an award-winning performance. Spent from spewing all my vitriol of society in general, I slumped to a heap in the leaves, panting for breath. It was while I lay there that I rolled over to one side and, looking up through the forest, spotted a man calmly standing way up in the fork of a nearby tree.

Puzzled, and more than just a little embarrassed, I sat up to get a better look. He wasn't really that close, maybe a hundred yards or so away, but I could make him out clearly. He was an older gentleman, probably in his forties or fifties. He was dressed in jeans and a plaid shirt and was also wearing a khaki-colored windbreaker or jacket and a gray fedora-style hat.

I dropped my head momentarily in embarrassment; then when I stood up, I could still see him, so for whatever reason, I started walking in that direction. I felt some sort of need to talk to the man—I guess, in a way, I felt like he was a part of the catharsis of the 'performance' I'd just put on for him in the woods. At least, if he was a near neighbor, I probably needed to convince him that the new farm owners didn't have a crazy daughter. At most, maybe he understood after listening to me rant (and isn't it really understanding that we all crave?), and he would turn out to be a good friend.

I went straight to the tree, only to find it empty. I walked all around the huge tree, inspecting it from every angle. I even called out, but the only response I received was the silence of the forest. Perplexed, I made my way back to my fairy circle. He must have made record time getting out of that tree from such a height, I mused. In order for him to have fled that fast, he must have thought I was bonkers!

I arrived back at the fairy circle and was twirling around when I glanced back up at his tree—and there he was again, in the same fork, way up near the top. I stood, hands on hips, and fixed him with my steadiest of gazes. He didn't move or acknowledge me in any form or fashion. Once again, I took off on a straight line for the tree...And once again, there was no man to be found when I arrived.

I was stymied. There was no place up in the tree he could hide. I even considered climbing the tree myself, but decided against it—something just didn't feel right. I went back to the clearing, and while casting sidelong glances so he wouldn't know I was watching, I saw him in the tree yet again. I just ignored him this time, and he was still up there when I left to walk back to the farmhouse.

I visited the fairy circle in the clearing on several occasions, but I only saw the man one other time, on the eve of my eighteenth birthday and also the last night I was ever at our farm. My mom sold it to some distant relations, and we have yet to go back and visit. I'm not sure just who or what the man in the tree is or represents—I kind of get the feeling he's someone who's passed away who used to live on the property. Perhaps even one of my relatives. He will always be special to me, and I feel kind of sad for him, a real melancholia for a spirit who remains in a tree only wishing he could interact once again with the living.

CHAPTER 62

THE CAT CARVING

I was playing in an old ditch beside the house I grew up in. I was probably all of ten years old. While climbing up one side of the ditch, I happened to spy a small hollow area underneath a tree root that was growing out over the top of the bank. Curious, I first poked into the little hidey-hole with a stick (to make sure there were no snakes or spiders or other creepy-crawly slithery things inside) and then explored it with my hand, all the while thinking this would be a great spot to stash something (as to what I would stash, I hadn't a clue, but it was a keen hiding spot nonetheless).

While clearing debris from the hole, I pulled out what looked and was shaped like half of a round river rock, as if it had been cut in two lengthwise. I started to toss it over my shoulder, but then something on the rock caught my eye—I saw the crudely drawn face of a cat staring back at me.

On closer examination, the 'rock' turned out to be half of an almost perfectly formed clay ball, into which someone had carved a classic (albeit simplistic) cat's face, complete with upside-down triangle nose and sporting sets of three whiskers on each side. Two small close-set eyes and two open-bottomed triangles for ears made up the whole of this handiwork.

Overjoyed at my fortune, I stuck the carving in my pocket and promptly forgot about it, as small boys are known to do. I didn't think about it until later in the night...when I started hearing strange noises in my house.

I was getting ready for bed and had absentmindedly tossed my clothing of the day on the floor of my closet—this was where my mom always looked for my stuff anyway, so I figured no harm, no foul. I turned on my small reading lamp and plopped into bed with a stack of comic books I had acquired earlier in the day from an older kid at school. Ah, ten-year-old boy bliss!

Just as I finished scanning the covers and had chosen a volume to peruse, I heard an odd scratching sound coming from somewhere in my room. I was puzzled, but didn't think much of it and happily continued to lose myself in the comic book.

A few minutes later, I heard the noise again. This time the scratching was more urgent, more fervent. It was if a small animal was trying to vie for my attention with the comic book. Granted, we did live out in the country and I had a few pets— but they all had their respective places outside and had never been allowed to set a paw within the confines of our farmhouse.

Diligently, I rose from the bed and began walking the periphery of the room, listening at all the windows and doors. Suddenly, it dawned on me—the sounds were coming from my closet. I eased over to the closet door and warily pressed an ear against it. Yep, sure enough, it sounded like something small and furry was gently but firmly trying to extricate itself from my closet.

I armed myself with a BB gun and a flashlight (I was ten years old, mind you) and quickly slid the door open on its track...

only to be met with a closet full of nothing. At least, nothing that wasn't supposed to be there. I didn't hear the scratching with the door open, but continued to poke around inside the closet with the barrel of the BB gun.

All of a sudden, when I shifted my blue jeans from the pile, the little carving I had found in the woods gently rolled out of the pants and came to rest upright on the floor. In the eerie beam of the flashlight, it appeared as if the little cat was glaring at me.

I resisted the urge to take the carving back immediately, settling instead to put it in the garage for the night. I didn't hear any more scratching, and when I got up the next day, I returned the little carved cat back to the hole in the woods where I had found it. Sometimes things are where they are for a very specific reason and are not meant to be disturbed by children.

CHAPTER 63

THE ACCIDENT

This happened to my dad and me on a lonely stretch of country road back in the '70s.

We were headed home after attending a car auction in a nearby town. It was really, really late—I'm guessing like 2 a.m. or so.

We came around a curve in the road, and my dad jammed on the brakes in our Monte Carlo. There was a white utility van sitting sideways in the road, blocking the way. The rear doors of the van were flung open wide, and an assortment of power tools were scattered all over the roadway.

There was also a bunch of fresh tree limbs and branches of various sizes in the road, leaves still attached. My dad backed up and tried to aim his headlights to get a better look. I was scanning the side of the road from my window, when I called out for my dad to stop backing up. We had almost backed into a motorcycle sitting on the shoulder of the road. We had initially not noticed the motorcycle because it, too, was covered by branches and brush.

I was leaning out the window, trying to decipher this weird scene, when I felt something wet splatter onto my hand. I pulled it back into the car and turned on the interior dome light, only to be startled out of my wits—my hand was spotted with droplets of fresh blood!

Now keep in mind, there was no one anywhere in sight—just a van sitting in the middle of the road, and a motorcycle on the shoulder. I suddenly had the most eerie feeling imaginable and told my dad that we needed to get out of there, and as fast as possible.

He agreed, thankfully, and was able to do a multiple-point turn and get the car turned around in the middle of the road, and we tore off down the road in the direction we had just come from. After about ten minutes of fast driving, we skidded to a stop in the gravel parking lot of an all-night diner. As luck would have it, there was a state trooper inside having a cup of coffee.

We went in and excitedly told our tale, and he agreed to follow us back to the location. I'd even shown him the large spatters of fresh blood on my hand before washing it off. All in all, I figure a ten-minute drive, five minutes explaining what we'd found, and then another fifteen-minute drive back to the spot on the road (naturally, my dad had chosen to drive slower with the state trooper following him, but I'm sure we still broke the speed limit).

We arrived at the bend in the road and...nothing was there. Save for a few of the fresh branches still scattered along the blacktop in the curve. No van, no tools, no motorcycle. The state trooper shined his super high beam light all around in the trees and woods, but other than being able to see where the branches had been freshly snapped and twisted off high above our heads (I'm estimating fifteen to twenty feet, if memory serves correctly), there was no evidence of anything having ever taken place on this dark stretch of road.

The trooper thanked us for our concern, told us to be careful, and climbed back in his cruiser and headed to the diner, I assume, to continue his coffee break. My dad and I got into our car and continued on toward home, the way being clear now. We never spoke about the incident, except years later when he mentioned it briefly and only then to concede that he still had no idea what it was that we saw.

Looking back, this is one of the creepiest things I have ever experienced. Had we happened upon a crime scene? An alien abduction? A ghostly replaying of some event from the past? How could it have been cleaned up so fast? I have no answers (but a million questions at least); however, the encounter did assist me in keeping an open mind about paranormal events and the unknown in general. I realized that no matter how wild the tale, the person could really be telling the truth and describing an incident just as it happened to them. Thank you for giving me the opportunity to tell about our encounter after all these decades.

CHAPTER 64

TREASURE FOUND AND LOST

When I was a kid, there was a man in our neighborhood named Charlie Tipton, who was a local entrepreneur and treasure hunter. He was successful at his endeavors and never held down an actual job (nor did he need to) as far as I knew. He was always finding lost or buried money, sometimes from caches that were hidden before the Civil War.

As Charlie himself was always fond of saying, treasure hunting often involves a bit of a supernatural element. Those old tales of a pirate killing a hapless shipmate so that his spirit would guard the treasure springs to mind.

Charlie had located a 'treasure map' retrieved from behind a stone in an old chimney he'd found in the woods where a house once stood.

Successfully deciphering the map, Charlie handily located the area and dug up the strongbox hidden decades previous. The curious thing was, the instant he pulled the strongbox from the ground, an old rusty, weed-encrusted tractor sitting in a nearby field roared to life.

As Charlie approached, the tractor belched smoke and fell silent once more. Charlie once stated that if he hadn't known better and hadn't trusted his senses so fully, he would have sworn he imagined the whole incident.

In addition to being a local treasure hunter, Charlie was known to be a treasure 'hider' as well—which only seems fitting, I suppose...

His sole heir, a son who was lame in one leg, wouldn't be able to scramble for hidden money the way Charlie had always managed to do, so Charlie supposedly hid an iron pot full of gold coins for his progeny. The son, whom I'll call Adam, worked the counter at a local feed store and spent the remainder of his life trying to find the wealth his father had hidden for him.

Although Charlie had secreted the aforementioned iron pot full of gold coins where his son would be able to retrieve it despite being partially crippled, Charlie, alas, passed away before taking time to leave a map or any form of instruction to Adam regarding where the wealth could be retrieved. Now, how's that for a quandary? The best treasure hunter in four counties didn't leave a map!

So, shorted of his inheritance, Adam managed to eke out a living at the feed store and spent his spare time imbibing alcohol and ranting about his father's lack of foresight. I can remember riding my bike by his house as a child, and being terrified of him when he was 'liquored up and pissed off,' as was said amongst us children. And who could blame him? I imagine I'd be upset too if I knew that somewhere a treasure cache—a pot full of gold coins—was waiting for me while I toiled away at manual labor to barely make ends meet...

Alas, poor Adam died as well, having never found his fortune. I heard later on that the container of coins was discovered, but that the finder (another area gentleman who was fond of searching with a metal detector) eventually went quite mad and had to be institutionalized—one of his claims was that he was being visited by ghosts claiming to own some of the items he had recovered.

CHAPTER 65

DISAPPEARING CEMETERY

This was out in the country in Rhode Island, and it happened around 1981, right after I had graduated from high school. I had gone to stay with relatives in Rhode Island, as my dad's work had taken him out of the country to France, and my mom luckily was able to go with him.

I had visited New England on a few occasions, but I was really enjoying my newfound freedom on this trip. It was nice to be a teen and not have your parents looking over your shoulder for a while. My relatives were not as overly cautious as my mom and dad, so that suited me just fine and took some of the pressure off those tasked with 'keeping an eye on me.'

While exploring in the woods a few miles down the road, I chanced across an old cemetery, forgotten and far off the beaten path. The stones were ancient and were some of the most ornate and intricately carved I had ever seen. As I was enjoying the handiwork associated with this now-lost art, I realized it was starting to get dark and I had better head back. Although I was having a blast being free, I didn't want to end up lost in an unfamiliar area after nightfall.

I went back a few days later to do some rubbings of the headstones, but could find no evidence that a cemetery had ever existed in that location. Perplexed, I pressed on, but eventually came to the bank of a shallow but fast-moving stream. The stream was unknown to me, so obviously I hadn't traveled this far before. I returned home with my beeswax and rice paper unused.

Later on that week, I even went to the county library and pulled out the dusty old topography maps, but even by going back several decades, I could not find any evidence of a cemetery having ever been located where I had been. I was certain it was the right area, due to the roadways, one of which had originally been a part of the route stagecoaches used centuries ago. I asked my relatives I was staying with, but none of the household knew anything about a cemetery nearby. Strange, strange, strange!

CHAPTER 66

THE PILE OF WALLETS

The creepiest thing that I ever came across in the woods was in New England during summer break. This would have been in either the very early '70s or very early '80s, while I was still in high school down South. I was up hiking in the woods near the river and was looking for a place to sit down for a spell and take a rest.

In a clearing not too far from the river, I came across a pile of wallets that appeared to be hastily hidden under some dead leaves.

Most of the wallets were rotten, but some looked newer than others. I poked around in them with a stick, and when one flopped open, I froze—inside were ID, credit cards and some moldering cash! I didn't check very thoroughly, but all of the wallets seemed to have personal effects left in them. I mean, for real—there were driver's licenses with people's pictures and stuff on them! Talk about stone-cold weird! All of a sudden, I got a very creepy sensation, as if I was being watched, so I took off back the way I came.

In retrospect, I probably should have alerted the authorities to this strange find. But I was only a teenager at the time and didn't always think or behave in the most rational, logical, or sensible manner. To this day, I have a nagging suspicion in the back of my mind that the wallets were deposited there by a serial killer—and if I had stuck around for much longer, my own wallet would have joined the forgotten pile.

CHAPTER 67

MOUNT BALDY

Mount Baldy is way up in the Badlands area of California. There are some legendary pipes up there, used to carry water down from the mountains and into constantly thirsty and drought-stricken Southern California. If you look in any of the skateboard magazines or search on YouTube, you can see skaters letting it all hang out in the giant full-pipes up on Baldy.

We would hitch rides to skate inside the huge tunnel-like drainage pipes on Baldy, but on this particular occasion we weren't successful in hitching a ride back home. Left with no alternative, we accepted our fate and began to prepare to sleep on Mount Baldy overnight. This far up in the mountains, it wasn't unusual to run into the odd rattlesnake now and then. (One skater we knew had actually been bitten by a rattler on Baldy. He survived, but the recovery took a long time, and he now has to permanently wear glasses because of the lasting effects of the snake venom.) So as we bedded down for the night, planning to walk out to the highway the next morning and see if we could hitch a ride with a tractor trailer driver, the odd happenings began. If you've never seen the water pipes on Mount Baldy, let me tell you—they are huge. Being as big as they are and made of concrete, the pipes produce a lot of strange echoes. Sounds will carry and seem to be coming from several different directions.

So here we are, a half dozen or so tough skate punks, sleeping outdoors in the mountains—when we start hearing all these weird voices. It was a mix of stuff, like people talking, kids laughing and also some electronic-sounding 'bleep bloop' type noises.

Crazy, huh? Well, there wasn't anything we could do. No way were we going to try to walk down from Baldy in the middle of the night. There were not any real shoulders on the road, and we would have either been greased by a big truck or had to plunge over the side to our deaths trying to leap out of harm's way.

The voices ebbed and flowed and finally let up just as dawn was breaking. My friends and I hadn't slept a wink, as the cacophony of noises and creepy goings-on had kept us awake all night. Bloodshot and bleary-eyed, we hitched a ride with an RV that happened along shortly after daybreak.

As we related our tale to the elderly driver and his wife, a vacationing retired couple from Scottsdale, Arizona, they allowed that they, too, believed the mountain to be haunted, and wouldn't have spent the night, even in the comfort and security of their RV, for love nor money.

CHAPTER 68

DEAN'S SHACK

Dean was a homeless (as far as I know) guy we used to hang out with while skateboarding. He seemed to live in a dilapidated shack way out in the woods. The shack had once been the ticket booth for a drive-in theater, although I have no idea why someone would have taken the time or energy to drag the little building way out in the woods in the absolute middle of nowhere.

When my friends and I were out skating during our elementary and middle school years, we would always make it a point to drop in and visit Dean. He was a fountain of knowledge about ghosts, conspiracy theories, girls and beer. He seemed ancient to us at the time, but I'm guessing he was probably only in his thirties.

There was always a stash of warm Pabst Blue Ribbon and *Playboy* magazines nearby, and although none of us partook of the beer, I can say those *Playboys* saw so much browsing action that they were literally falling apart and were very, very dog-eared.

During the summer before I started eighth grade, Dean passed away. He was decapitated in a car accident while hitch-hiking his way back from town (I don't know for sure, but I'd be willing to bet he was on a beer run), and after that, anytime we ventured back in the woods to Dean's shack, we would experience some sort of paranormal or supernatural activity.

Sometimes it might be laughter, just barely audible, and other times a soft, crying sound. It sounded like Dean to us, and even to this day thinking back on it makes the hairs stand up on my arms and on the back of my neck.

We eventually got to the point where we would go back to Dean's shack, but refused to go inside. However, the creep factor and strange goings-on continued to escalate beyond that, and I'd say by a year after his death, we wouldn't go near the shack at all.

To the best of my knowledge, it's probably still sitting out there in the woods, if it hasn't rotted into the ground yet. I don't think Dean was trying to scare us, but instead believe his spirit was sad and lonely and was just trying to reach out to us for company—which would mean that Dean was the same in death as he had been in life. Rest in peace, Dean, rest in peace.

CHAPTER 69

THE LITTLE MAN

When I was a kid, we saw something in the woods that scared the crap out of us. It was some sort of—well, the only way I can describe it is it was a little man. We could never agree on just what it was. Maybe it was an alien, a leprechaun or an elf of some sort, however, we did agree that it resembled a little man. I'd say he was about double the size of a two-liter soda bottle, although there was even some disagreement on that—it was like we all saw the same thing, but we didn't see the same thing, ya know? I hope that makes some sense...

My friend Jimmy and I were playing in a big ditch that was overgrown with weeds. I'm not really sure whose property it was on, so we were probably trespassing, but we were just kids, so we really didn't worry about it. The general rule of thumb when you're a kid is that if you're on someone's property and they don't want you there, they will come out and scream at you until you leave.

So anyway, we were playing in the ditch. It was full of

weeds and vines and junk and stuff; it was probably pretty dangerous. But it was where the whole neighborhood played. On any given day, there might be as many as a dozen kids all total in the ditch. It stretched for probably a half mile or so, so there was plenty of room for everyone to stretch out and do their own thing.

On this particular day, however, and for whatever reason, the only kids who were in the ditch were me and Jimmy. Looking back, I'm thinking we probably skipped school that day and that's the reason we were the only ones there at the time. We would have been all of about ten years old, so yeah, that sounds about right.

I don't remember exactly what we were doing when we saw him, but Jimmy saw him first. He didn't say anything, but I just remember it was kind of quiet, and I looked up from whatever I was doing (probably digging up old bottles—people had thrown trash in the ditch for decades, and it wasn't unusual for us to find old bottles dating back to the early 1900s) and caught sight of Jimmy's surprised look on his face.

I stopped whatever I was doing and stood up so that I could see over the weed growth to whatever had Jimmy transfixed. I know it sounds crazy, but what he was looking at was a little man who couldn't have been more than a couple of feet tall. He looked like one of those concrete garden gnomes come to life, minus the stocking cap. He was wearing darkish green and beige loose-fitting clothing, and he had shoulder-length white hair and a trim little white beard.

The scariest thing, though, (as if a tiny man wasn't scary enough) was the angry look on his face—he was pissed off! I'm not sure if he saw us or not, but by this time Jimmy's paralysis of initial fright had broken, and he let loose with something between a cry and a wail that made the hair stand up on my arms.

I had been curious at first, but Jimmy's scream did something to me. I started screaming too, and we both started running down the ditch line for all we were worth. We ran all the way to Jimmy's house and waited for someone to get home so we could get in. The first person home was Jimmy's older brother Toby, who was in high school and therefore fearless in our ten-year-old eyes. We recounted our harrowing experience, and Toby looked at us like we were trying to pull his leg. I think though that our sincerity finally showed, and he realized we were truly frightened. He said, "Come on, let's go," and made us go back to the ditch with him.

Jimmy and I were both still too scared to go back down in the ditch, so instead we stood and pointed at the other side of the bank where we'd seen the little man parting through the weeds and making his way down. There were even some fresh skid marks in the dirt and grass on the bank that looked like tiny footprints, like feet about the size of a small potato.

Other than that, we didn't see anything. We had heard stories about stuff in the ditch, but that was usually just kids fooling around. I don't recall anyone else ever having seen a little man. Toby joked that since kids were always finding discarded girlie magazines in the ditch, maybe the little man was angry that we kids had found his secret stash.

It was a while before we played in the ditch again, and when we did, we always kept an eye out for the little man. We never did see him again, but to this day, whenever I pass by that ditch, I always wonder what it was we saw that day as kids. I never see any kids playing in there these days, so I guess times have really changed. Maybe the little man is still in there somewhere, thumbing through a dog-eared copy of *Playboy* from decades ago and wondering where all the kids went.

CHAPTER 70

RAIN OF MARBLES

Now, I'm going to tell on myself a little here—you're not supposed to ever ask a lady her age, but if you are smart, you can figure out about how old I am. This was back in the day when children, schoolkids, still played with marbles—it was a grand deal at the time—so now you know that I'm simply ancient!

Mind you, back then we didn't have a lot of entertainment—television was years away, a radio was a large appliance in your living room, and most kids around where we lived didn't have a lot of toys. Marbles kind of made up for that. A rousing game of marbles was considered a fun time by one and all. Every child in my school had a collection of marbles, and every day on the playground at school, you could find several games in motion. Your marbles were your pride and joy, and you knew every one in your collection.

I told you all that to tell you this—I was out in the woods near our farm in Gallatin, Tennessee, where I grew up. It was a sunny, clear day in the early summer—there wasn't a cloud in the sky. I was walking along, picking berries from wild bushes that grew down by the creek on the back side of our property. It wasn't anything for us kids to play miles away from the house back then—there wasn't much real danger out in the country, at least not like there is these days.

As I was walking along, putting berries in a tin lard bucket I had brought along for the purpose, I felt something hit me on the shoulder. I swatted my hand at the air, at first thinking it might be a bee—there were bumblebees around in the summer, and they were capable of stinging the fire out of you! I didn't see any bee, but what I did see on the ground, just as proud as a rooster, was a shiny blue marble.

I gleefully picked up the marble and pocketed it in my dress. A fine addition to my personal collection. Plus, 'finders keepers, losers weepers,' as we used to say! While smiling smugly at the thought of my new treasure, I heard a muffled sound as something struck the ground beside me...It was another marble!

All different kinds, from a clear, blue sky. One initially pinged me in the head, I thought it was a rock or maybe a hail-stone, but on closer inspection it turned out to be a glass marble and was rather warm to the touch. They continued to fall for about the next hour, sporadically. There was no cover that anyone could have hid behind to launch the projectiles, and furthermore, they appeared to be falling straight down, whereas they would have fallen along an arc or angle if fired from the ground.

Years later, as I was thinking about this strange occurrence, I discovered the writings of Charles Fort, the father of 'Forteana,' which is the study of odd happenings. In his seminal work, *The Book of the Damned*, Fort wrote about such similar 'rains,' although his usually were about small frogs, fish or slivers of fresh meat. All in all, I think I'd rather be hit with marbles than any of the above!

CHAPTER 71

THE ABANDONED CAROUSEL

I came across a strange thing in the woods once—something very, very strange. It was an old carousel that had been hauled into the woods after some children were severely injured on it. I don't want to give away the exact location, because I'd feel bad if someone else went looking for it and got hurt themselves. I'll just say that it's in the area of the southern United States and leave it at that...

I had been out geocaching and just happened to take the long way back to my truck. I knew I couldn't get lost as long as I had my trusty GPS unit, so I was taking my time and just enjoying being out in the woods on a warm fall day—with winter coming on, I wanted to get as much outdoor time in before it got too cold to enjoy it.

I was working my way around a huge clump of overgrowth I'd encountered, when something caught my eye inside the brush. As it turned out, I was seeing a carousel horse staring back at me. That explained the large clump of overgrowth!

There's something eerie about a carousel that's shut down anyway, and the creep factor goes up by at least a hundred when that carousel is abandoned in pieces deep in the woods. I have experienced the feeling of being watched when deep in the woods on many occasions, but this one took the cake.

I took one last look around, expecting to see someone peering back from the shadows (which, thankfully, I did not) and then fled back to my truck. I was overcome with a deep feeling of despair and sadness.

Over the next couple of weeks, I couldn't get the image of the creepy carousel out of my head, so eventually I went to the big county library and did some research. Not surprisingly, I finally managed to uncover the history of the carousel—it had been scrapped and hauled into the woods after one child was killed on it and several more injured by it in the early 1960s in another part of the state. I haven't been back and can't say that I ever will be. I feel that the spirit of the dead child must have attached itself to the old wooden carousel. I told you it was a very strange thing.

CHAPTER 72

MYSTERIOUS SPHERE

I grew up near Oak Ridge, Tennessee, so that little bit of information will hopefully make my story a little less nonsensical—if you know anything about Oak Ridge and the Manhattan Project during World War II, you know that a lot of interesting technology was developed at the Oak Ridge National Laboratory (aka the X-10 facility).

This particular day, I had been out fishing along the banks of Melton Hill Lake in the Solway community, which is just a few miles outside Oak Ridge. The area where I was at was just across the river from Oak Ridge National Laboratory.

While waiting for a fish to take the bait, I observed a strange occurrence on the opposite bank—I saw something shiny and metallic moving swiftly along the shore, more or less even with my position.

The object appeared to be a sphere or ball made of dull, semi-reflective metal and probably measuring eighteen to twenty-four inches tall/round. If there was anyone nearby controlling it, they would have been visible, as there were only weeds growing down on the lake bank—TVA [the Tennessee Valley Authority] had recently bushhogged the bottoms, so there were neither weeds nor woods deep enough where a human being could have been hidden.

The 'ball' (as I'll just call it for brevity) would amble along the lakeshore, first this way then that, as if it were searching for something. As it darted to and fro, at various speeds, I noticed that it would always skitter back just short of actually going in the water.

There was no one anywhere nearby who could have been controlling the object. I also knew, from messing with radio-controlled airplanes when I was a kid, that there was no way the thing had an antenna.

After watching the ball roll around the edge of the water for the better part of an hour, it suddenly seemed as if it suddenly remembered an important appointment and took off in the other direction, towards the National Laboratory. Unfortunately, as I was on the other side of the lake, I couldn't follow suit. The last time I spotted it, it was rolling through the tall grass, up a slight incline. I have no rational explanation for this event.

CHAPTER 73

STANDING STONES

This is a story about some standing stones that I came across in the woods of Alabama. While they are not as fancy as England's famous Stonehenge, I think they may have been even older, predating even the Native Americans, based on my own personal beliefs and research.

I'm not going to give out the exact location, as there are some people now conducting serious research at the site, and I don't want it to be covered in graffiti, littered with beer cans, or used for heavy metal 'Satan parties'—I'm sure you understand...

I've been working on my aforementioned personal theory about such places, not only in the United States, but throughout the world. I think it dates back to biblical times and the Tower of Babel, and also relates to the pyramids throughout the world, such as those in Egypt and on the North and South American continents.

If you read in the Bible, the people were trying to build a tower to heaven, sort of in arrogance to God. Well, in Genesis,

God came down and confused their language and scattered them across the earth...

Now think about this for a moment—you're building a tower, and suddenly—in the blink of an eye—you find yourself in another part of the world. Talk about having your mind completely blown! Now, under those circumstances—and remember that these were primitive people—what would you do?

I think they did what was natural...They were building a tower and then suddenly found themselves in an unknown location...so they might have ascertained, "Well, we were building a tower and suddenly ended up here. Maybe if we build another tower, we'll be able to go back!"

And in a nutshell, that's my explanation of Stonehenge, of the pyramids in Peru, Mexico and Egypt, and the 'standing stones' and strange 'monoliths' found throughout the world.

Again, it's just my own personal theory based on what I've read, but it makes just as much sense to me as any other theory I've heard posited. Maybe more sense than most, come to think about it. Give it some thought and see what you think...

CHAPTER 74

LOST SOLDIER

While only sort of 'in the woods,' I had an encounter once that defied explanation on several different levels. It was back in 1990, and I was living in Fort Oglethorpe, Georgia, and dating a girl who lived just across the state line in Chattanooga, Tennessee. I was a young buck, all of eighteen, and knew everything—or at least I thought I did. I had an old pickup truck, a part-time job in a grocery store, and ruled the earth back then.

It was Tuesday night (my 'weekend' or days off were Tuesday and Wednesday back then), and I had been in Chattanooga spending time with my sweetheart. Our day had consisted of going around to the Fort Oglethorpe and Chickamauga areas and seeing what we could find around those old battlefields.

Now, if you grew up in the area where we both lived, you would know that there have been stories since the Civil War (and supposedly even some prior) about all the ghostly goings-on around Chickamauga battlefield. Now it's a national park and amusement area, but back during the Civil War, it was home to one of the bloodiest battles ever, apart from Gettysburg.

One of the most popular (and mind-bendingly scary) legends revolves around areas of the battlefield known as Snodgrass Hill and Wilder Tower. The story goes that even while the battle was going on, a weird apparition with glowing green eyes was seen moving among the dead and dying soldiers from both sides of the conflict. Known as 'Ol' Green Eyes,' the figure is still seen in modern times, with even respectable (and sober) park rangers claiming to have had sightings of the mysterious beast.

There's also a haunting perpetrated by a 'lady in white,' who is said to be the spirit of a Civil War bride who searches the battlefield eternally for her young husband, who never returned home from battle.

On this particular evening, along about twilight, the sighting I had was neither of the known haunts—my sighting was unique. I was driving up Alexander Bridge Road, which essentially cuts all the way across the northeastern side of the battlefield. Like I said, it was almost dark, and we hadn't seen anyone in the last couple of hours. The rangers don't step up their patrols until full dark when the park closes and they want to make sure everyone has left.

I'm also aware of the occasional re-enactors who frequent the park, but there wasn't any reenactment going on that day (and certainly not into the night), so that makes my sighting all the more unusual.

Just as we rounded the bend where Alexander Bridge Road connects with Lafayette Road, I caught sight of someone just out of the range of the car's headlights. I slowed to a stop and pointed out the figure to my date. She immediately got goosebumps and insisted that we leave the area ASAP. But before I could react, my eyes locked with those of what we were seeing— a gaunt, pale Confederate soldier. We stared at each other for a few seconds, and then the phantom turned away and, with more than a hint of pathos, marched into the woods off to the edge of the clearing. Had I just come face-to-face with the spirit of a long-dead Confederate soldier?

With that, the spell broke and we tore willy-nilly out of there and back for Chattanooga just as hard as we could go. My girlfriend had a hard time sleeping, and I stayed up with her, not going to sleep until well after the sun had risen the next morning.

When we finally did awaken, I pondered the strange encounter of the night before. What was the reason the soldier had revealed himself to us? Was it (as my girlfriend feared) a warning of some sort from the netherworld? Had it been a warning, but actually for another reason? I often wonder that if I had never had the encounter, I would have left Chattanooga a lot earlier the next morning—and possibly have been involved in one of the most deadly multiple-car pile-ups in US history: The crash on Interstate 40 near the Bowaters Plant in South Pittsburg, Tennessee, killed fifteen people on December 12, 1990, when seventy-five vehicles crashed due to poor visibility in the early morning fog...If that truly is the case, then I owe the old soldier a huge thank-you for possibly saving my life.

CHAPTER 75

GIANT EYES

This happened in Jefferson National Forest when I was a boy. My friends and I had gone up to that area of the state to hike a bit of the Appalachian Trail. We had taken the trail as far as Damascus, Virginia, and stopped at a roadside market for supplies. After filling our packs and canteens, we had taken off again on a nearby trailhead known as the Virginia Creeper Trail.

It wasn't exactly a spot where camping was permitted, but we pitched our tent there anyway—better to beg for forgiveness than to ask for permission...at least sometimes, right?

So our little clandestine camp was set up; we had some grub stealthily warmed over cans of Sterno and settled in for the night. It was all well and good, just some friends camping out beneath the stars, about to drift off to sleep after a long day of hiking—and then all hell broke loose.

It started out as noises, like some kind of wild animal. Now, my friends and I were not only Boy Scouts, but a bunch of farm boys from the mountains of upper east Tennessee...We knew our way around the woods, having grown up in them, and we knew the creatures in those woods. And these noises were unlike anything that any of us had ever heard before (or since).

Describing the sounds as yips, yowls and growls is like calling the Queen Mary a boat—words just aren't enough. At this point, we were all fully awake and unsure of either the direction or source of the sound. Whatever it was, it was big, pissed off, and headed in our general direction—in the pitch black of a moonless night, deep in a national forest and miles away from anyone who might help us should the need arise.

As the grunts and growls grew closer, so did the sound of crashing timbers and broken branches. I don't think an elephant would have made as much noise coming through the brush. I'm sure I speak for the other fellows when I say that all the hair on my neck and arms was standing up at this point, and I felt like it wouldn't take much to make me wet my pants—now that's how truly scared I was at the time!

We finally managed to gather outside the tent, more or less in a circle with our backs touching, flashlights in hand. We played the beams over the surrounding woods to try to ascertain what was making such a commotion. For the most part, however, the beams were too weak to be of much use in illuminating the dense growth of forest.

We noticed that the crashing and thrashing had abated, and we held our breath as the quiet stillness of the forest returned. If anything, it was too quiet—I think that was even more frightening. I continued to shine my light into the surrounding woods, when suddenly a reflection caught my eye.

I moved the beam of the flashlight back over the area, and there it was again—two giant eyes glowing an eerie red!

Unable to speak for a moment due to fear, I managed to make a squeak and get the other guys' attention.

"What in the hell is that thing?" one of my friends exclaimed, only to be met with gasps of disbelief and an otherwise continued silence.

Looking back, the smartest thing to do would probably have been for all of us to run—but I stood my ground—I wanted to see what this thing was that was vexing us.

While I've read lots of Bigfoot encounters since that time, I have to wonder…Mine is the only one I'm aware of where 'Bigfoot' had a set of red glowing eyes. The only creature or cryptid I'm aware of that fits this bill is the infamous Mothman of West Virginia and Ohio. Granted, we weren't really THAT far from West Virginia…It makes me wonder just what we encountered in those woods.

CHAPTER 76

THE CRYING GRAVE

Out in an abandoned area of North Georgia, there's a grave located in the family plot of an old homesite where nothing remains except bits of the foundation and the crumbling remnants of a stone chimney.

My personal knowledge of the grave began during my days in elementary school. I always enjoyed hearing spooky stories, like every kid, but I never put a lot of stock into them as I got older. It's funny how something you take as the absolute gospel when you are a child can seem so childish when you are older. But I digress...

As expected, it was around Halloween, and stories of haunted places and creepy happenings were the order of the day on the asphalt playground. One story I kept hearing repeated really gave me the chills—it was about a spooky, abandoned cemetery in the woods (which, in and of itself, is good scare fodder) where the sound of either a woman or a young girl could be heard weeping.

My best friend, Richard, and I were diehards when it came to anything weird or creepy. We had spent literally several summers hunting for Bigfoot in the woods, scanning the night skies for UFOS, and exploring old houses and buildings for ghosts. Naturally, we decided a trip in order to check out the grave was the best course of action.

We synchronized our stories—his mom thought he was spending the night with me, and my mom thought I was spending the night with him—and off to the graveyard we flew on our bikes one dark Friday night.

Nowadays (and probably back then if we'd only known), the biggest danger was the cars tearing by on the expressway, oblivious to two kids pedaling along (equally oblivious) on the shoulder of the highway. We ambled along and eventually arrived at the location where the 'Crying Grave' was supposed to exist.

The going was a considerable degree tougher than we had initially anticipated. What started out as an okay gravel road eventually dwindled down to a trail, then a footpath, then an even smaller throughway, which kids in the neighborhood referred to as a goat path or a game trail. The sides of the path were so overgrown that we had to dismount our bicycles and push them ahead of ourselves.

A lot of the weeds we were wading through in the dark turned out to be (as we would find out later...the hard way) poison ivy. The mosquitoes, blue bottles, no-see-ums and whatever else could fly and bite were having a field day—we were a warm-blooded buffet in the woods.

After what seemed like forever (a half hour at least), the goat path opened out into a large clearing. The moon had moved out from behind the clouds, and we could see the lone tombstone off on the edge of the almost perfectly formed circle of the clearing.

The stone was so old and weather worn that the name and

dates had faded out of existence decades before either of us had been born. We played our flashlights over the stone as well as over the deep, dark surrounding woods outside the clearing. While it was very, very spooky, I got the distinct feeling that it was so far out in the sticks that even the ghosts were unaware of the locale. That all changed within the space of a few minutes...

It started out as a low moaning sound, kind of like what it sounds like if you blow across the top of an empty glass cola bottle—sort of a drawn-out whooooooo whooooooo. My friend and I looked at each other, eyes growing wide in disbelief. If I looked even half as scared as my friend did to me, then we were obviously frightened out of our wits! In almost perfect unison, we clicked off our flashlights, thinking that the darkness would serve to hide us from whatever was making the moaning noise.

Although hidden from sight, the source of the noise continued. It rose in volume and pitch and got to the point where it was more of a crying noise. I think I almost soiled myself with unbridled fear. We decided we'd had enough, so we clambered aboard our bikes and fled in the other direction as if our heads were on fire.

After we cleared the immediate area, we slowed down from our fever-pitched ride. Stopping to catch our breath, we were startled to hear the noise again—that's right, the crying noise seemed to be following us out of the woods—now, we had even more reason to flee for our very lives!

Every time we would think it was safe and stop to keep from passing out from sheer exertion, the noise would start up again, first distant and then closer and closer. Eventually, after this creepy game of cat and mouse, we reached the dreaded expressway. If anyone had bothered to notice, two panicked kids on Schwinn Stingray bicycles must have been a funny sight.

Needless to say, we made it back, and the ghost or whatever it was didn't follow us home (that was another part of the rumor or legend), and we never heard the noise again. And, not being ones to push our luck, we never went back. I wouldn't ever go there even now as an adult. We did get some good mileage out of our tale on the schoolyard playground though—I'm sure there are still kids who shiver at our story of the infamous nighttime bike ride to the Crying Grave of Catoosa County.

CHAPTER 77

BULL'S BREATH

I was out hunting early one morning on a neighboring farm out in the wilds of Virginia. The farm was no longer in operation, and I had permission from the current owners. There wasn't any neighbors for miles around, just woods and trees and what seemed like miles and miles of overgrown fields. To me it seemed like the perfect place to hunt any small game that might be in season.

I had walked past some of the dilapidated outbuildings and was waist high in the weeds when I came upon what I believed to be an old, disused well house or springhouse. Back in the days before refrigeration, people used springhouses and deep water wells to keep things like milk and butter cold and preserved.

As I waded through the weeds up to the springhouse, I noticed a strange mist hovering in the air just to one side of the old boarded walls. The sun was just barely shining over the hills, so it seemed to give the vapor an almost golden glow...At least I assumed it was the sun.

Now the worrisome thing about this is that the farm was disused—I mean as in completely abandoned, no people or farm animals had been here on the premises in at least two decades if not longer. Suddenly I realized that if the mist I was seeing was a bull blowing its breath out between the slats of the spring-house (which had been my first impression), then I (and possibly the bull as well) was in deep, deep trouble. I wasn't entirely comfortable with shooting someone's livestock, but I was rather attached to my own hide as well—if it came down to either me or the bull...well, you get the idea.

I slowly raised my rifle, took aim, and stepped around the corner of the springhouse—to be met with absolute nothingness. There was nary a thing inside, at least not a living one. To this day, I believe I saw someone's ghost beside that old springhouse, perhaps a long-dead farmer wondering what I was doing on his land. I never went hunting there again.

CHAPTER 78

VAPOR MAN

While driving at night, I came around a curve in the road in a heavily wooded area. Much to my consternation, I braked hard and swerved to the left to avoid a man who was standing directly in the roadway. However, the 'man' wasn't a man at all, but rather some form of apparition, seemingly made out of mist or vapor.

I had a really fast Chevrolet Camaro at the time, and I had been driving what was in reality way too fast for the little country roads I was traveling on. I jammed on the brakes, too late, of course, to avoid missing the figure, and skidded right through it. My Camaro came to rest on the high side of the curve, partially in the weeds.

I leapt out, expecting to find a crushed, mangled body on the side of the road, my heart pounding ninety miles an hour. As I started to calm down a bit, it began to dawn on me—I hadn't hit a thing—there was no crash, nor was there any damage to my pride and joy Camaro. I stood there scratching my head until a very uneasy feeling began to creep over me.

It was if something was telling me I needed to get back in my car and get out of there—NOW—but at a sensible pace... Which was exactly what I did. Was it a ghost? A warning not to drive so fast? An omen? I don't guess I'll ever know, but it seems to have done the job, whatever the job was.

CHAPTER 79

ISLAND OF THE WITCHES

Siquijor is an island in the South China Sea off the coast of Cebu in the Philippines. While working overseas in a contract position, I had the opportunity to visit the island firsthand and experience the supernatural activity that has long been rumored to occur there.

I saw one man who had life-sized 'paper dolls' made out of newspaper. He laid them out on the floor of a nipa hut and then started waving a little stick or wand around. Shortly, the two paper figures began to stir, gently at first, but then more and more. Eventually, they were standing completely up and dancing around inside the hut. This continued for several minutes, like fifteen minutes or so, and then the figures airily floated down to rest on the floor once more. I'm not sure if it was witchcraft or some very clever sleight of hand, but it was a very, very creepy thing to observe nonetheless.

I also heard of a kangaroo-looking animal of some sort that would bound around on the island after darkness. Now, as if I need to tell you, kangaroo are not native to the Philippine Islands—I suppose someone could have imported one to the island from Australia and turned it loose, but it's still scary to think about some big, weird, hairy animal out jumping around in the darkness!

In addition to all the paranormal oddities, there were rumors of rather mundane—yet completely sinister—acts being perpetrated. I was told by some locals in Cebu City (on the neighboring island of Cebu, a short ride via air boat from Siquijor) that it wasn't unheard of even in recent years for visitors to be kidnapped and held for ransom (although I understand this can happen anywhere in the Philippines—it actually happened to an American expat friend of mine in Manila). Another little 'trick' the inhabitants of Siquijor like to play is to poison the food of foreigners...and then offer you the antidote for a healthy sum of pesos—a nice racket, I suppose, if you can get away with it.

Although I was neither kidnapped (my friend in Manila was able to ransom himself for the cash he had on his person, approximately two hundred US dollars, although the joke was on the kidnappers—he told them he had no family in the states who would ransom him—but he was actually the only child of an only child, and his extremely wealthy, and doting, grandmother would have easily and readily paid millions of greenbacks for his safe return), nor poisoned (I hired some locals as my 'food tasters,' thus preventing any chicanery with my eats—I had heard the 'poison' and resultant 'antidote' were, indeed, fake —but who'd be willing to bet their very life on it?) I did experience some unusual activity on Siquijor and plan to return there someday to film a documentary about the island and the strange goings-on that occur there.

CHAPTER 80

ALIEN RESISTANCE

I was camping near the river, and on the second night, I began to have strange, very disturbing dreams. By the third night, I was becoming more and more convinced that there was more than meets the eye going on. I decided to steel myself and prepare to fight back—I would resist the aliens—I refused to allow myself to be abducted!

How do you fight a foe that supposedly doesn't exist? I had read all the books about alien abduction, and one of the things that struck me as a constant through everyone's tale is that NO ONE tried to fight back! There was my answer! If I flatly refused to be abducted—if I fought back tooth and nail, then maybe—just maybe—I could prevail against the alien threat...

By refusing to make myself available, by refusing to go along like a sheep led to the slaughter for their nightmarish and horrific 'tests,' then maybe I could get some peace and be left alone by the entities.

I was prepared that night when I finally lay down and

allowed myself to drift off to sleep. I slept the tired but deep sleep of the righteously angry—let them come and try to start something with me—I dared them!

It wasn't long before I felt the old familiar sting—I heard the tones and felt the paralysis begin to take hold. In my mind, my pep talk began: I don't have to accept this—I won't accept this—I refuse to accept this!

Slowly, I felt their presence enter the area. As usual there were three or four of them. Suddenly, I realized I wasn't paralyzed—I broke free and stood. Although I found it somewhat disconcerting to find that I was no longer safe and secure I wasn't surprised—they had to take me elsewhere to do whatever it is they do—tests, probing, experiments...

I had faked the paralysis well, but now I had had enough as they approached on each flank. I sat up on the bed or table or whatever it was where they had me, and it startled them. I used this moment—this element of surprise as it were—to launch my attack. I grabbed the one nearest to me by his long, slender neck and twisted for all I was worth. Incredibly, I felt the neck twist in my hands, it was very soft, like twigs covered in plush fabric, but smooth instead of furry or even scaly. There was a sickening crunch and the alien went limp. Its huge black eyes looked at me, unbelievingly, and then filmed over and closed. I couldn't help but notice it had two sets of eyelids—one on the bottom and one on the top.

The other figures froze and I hesitated and then dropped the dead one I was holding. *Why did you do this?* I heard in my head. *What have you done?*

"Go ahead, try me!" I screamed, reaching for the next one nearest me (which skittered away just out of reach). "I'll kill you—I'll kill all of you!"

They clearly weren't expecting this sudden turn of events. They all withdrew into a clump and stood close together, obviously deciding what to do next and how to handle this crazy earthling who had already killed one of their own and was threatening the rest with at least grievous bodily harm, if not certain death.

They seemed to have elected one of them as a 'representative,' and he/she/it (do they have a sex? Intersex?) approached me somewhat petulantly. As this one approached, the other two dragged the one I had killed out of the circular, gray steel room.

The representative stood looking at me, and I caught what I considered at the time to be a hint of pathos in those big black eyes. Again, I felt (more than heard) the words *What have you done? Why did you do this? How could you do this?* echo through my head and my psyche. At first I did feel a tinge of remorse, but then my rage—my anger at being taken against my will, my rage at being violated—resurfaced and bile and bitterness spewed forth. In my mind, I screamed at the creature. I called it every manner of obscenity I had ever heard before.

It tried talking back, trying to tell me 'but we have the right,' but I wouldn't back down or let it force its thoughts into my brain—I wasn't about to back down now. "You have NO RIGHT," I screamed in my mind. "What makes you think you HAVE THE RIGHT?"

Instead of responding or trying to argue, it suddenly began to slip backwards—it was if it was moving without moving, if you can imagine that. Then I realized that the alien wasn't moving—I was. I was slowly slipping backwards; then the sense of motion grew faster and faster. I heard a loud POP and was then in complete darkness. I blinked a couple of times, and then found myself, oddly enough, alone It was quiet—I could hear the night chirps of crickets outside.

Had they given up on me? Had killing one of them been the last straw? Would they punish me or let me go—perhaps find a more pliable and willing subject to cater to their probing and examination whims and desires.

Whatever happened, it seems to have been the end of my alien abduction experiences, at least for now. I no longer dream of aliens, and I haven't had a night terror abduction experience in over three years. Sometimes, it's best to fight back—you never know what you are capable of until you have nothing left to lose.

CHAPTER 81

LAUGHING CHILDREN

Well, this was sort of out in the woods—it was in a huge prefab metal building out in the middle of the woods in the middle of nowhere. I was working the graveyard shift for a tool and plumbing supply company that had the contract for a large processing plant. The plant ran twenty-four hours a day, but, fittingly enough, only ran a skeleton crew on the graveyard shift. The contract required that someone be on-site at the suppliers area twenty-four hours a day, and I was lucky enough to get the graveyard shift, which I enjoyed—it was nice to virtually have the place to myself, only occasionally being disturbed if someone from processing needed a particular tool or fixture.

Most nights I would read or surf the internet on the company computer, but on this particular night I turned the lights off save for a small desk lamp, and leaned back in my chair to catch a few winks. Just as I started to doze off, I had a very distinct impression that someone was watching me. *Let 'em watch*, I thought. If they didn't have anything better to do than watch me sleep, then bully for them.

As I began to doze, I heard small distinct voices. Children, female, at least three or four of them total. For some reason, instead of bolting wide awake and going to check out the source of the voices, I instead continued to rest. I felt very relaxed and pleasant. The voices got louder and louder, and shortly it sounded like I was surrounded. At this point, the voices began to sing a song, a nursery rhyme I believe, and they were distinctly moving around me in a circle. I simply smiled and listened to the beautiful singsong voices of the little girls, and they danced 'round and 'round me in my comfy chair.

CHAPTER 82

WHAT DID WE RUN OVER?

This was back in the mid-1970s. My family lived in Scottsboro, Alabama, at the time, and we had driven up into East Tennessee to visit some relatives—my grandma lived up there at the time, as well as several of my aunts and uncles.

On this particular trip, my mom and dad and I were in one car, and my sister and her husband and young son were following along behind us in their vehicle. It wasn't a long drive, maybe two to three hours, if memory serves correct.

We had just crossed out of Alabama and into Tennessee, and I believe it was about two or three in the morning—it was indeed after midnight, I do remember that much. The place we were driving through was kind of swampy, just a narrow two-lane road out in the middle of nowhere.

Suddenly and without any warning, we hit something rather large with our car. My dad was driving and was talking to my mom, so neither one of them really saw what happened, although my dad is really good at watching the highway. The only thing I can figure is that way out here in the middle of nowhere, he let his guard down a little—my dad is proud of the fact that in all his decades and decades of driving, he has never had an accident and has never had any sort of traffic ticket or moving violation.

I was sitting on the edge of the back seat, sort of leaning over the front seat, having been engaged in conversation with my mom and dad. I no longer recall what we were discussing, but I was politely listening when we hit whatever it was. All I remember seeing was a dark shadowbox two to three feet high dart in front of the car from the shoulder on the right-hand side of the road. There was a heavy bang as the car and the object impacted, and the car even rocked a bit on its chassis.

"What was that?" my dad asked, slowing the car. He looked both in the rearview mirror as well as out his window backwards, but didn't see anything. "Might have been a deer," he mused as he continued driving. My sister's husband was driving right behind us in their car, and they didn't react as if anything was amiss, so we just kept driving. The rest of the drive was spent discussing what it was we might have hit, and we were soon pulling into my uncle's driveway near Knoxville. I'm guessing it was about a half hour to forty-five minutes that we continued driving after we hit the thing.

When we pulled in, my uncle was waiting up for us, and he came out through the garage door and turned on the floodlights on the front of his house, which illuminated our cars in his paved driveway.

"Jim," my uncle Bill called to my dad as he stared at the front of our car, "what in the world did you hit? There's blood all over the front of your car. It looks like gallons of it!"

I ran around to the front of the car, and, sure enough, there was blood all over the front of the car—it's on the chromed bumper, it's on the grill, it's on the headlights, it's on the air dam and ground effects pieces under the bumper, there are even some streaks down the side of the car and across the hood—it was lots and lots of blood.

My dad just stood and stared with his mouth open. It was easy to see that he was very upset. He began talking to my sister's husband, Bobby, who had walked to the front of our car and was shaking his head in abject disbelief as well.

"I saw something," Bobby said conspiratorially, while making sure my mom and sister didn't overhear. "I think it could have been a big dog or some other animal—but you know what I thought it was at first glance? A guy in a scuba diving suit, a wet suit, crawling across the road on all fours."

I watched all the color visibly drain from my dad's face.

"We have to go back," he whispered to Bobby. "We have to see for sure."

Bobby nodded in agreement and said something to my uncle Bill, who helped my mom and sister and my sister's little boy in the house. After the last of the things were carried in, the four of us (Uncle Bill, Bobby, my dad and myself) all hopped into Bobby's station wagon and stealthily drove back in the direction from which we'd come. It was still very late (or very early, I guess, depending on your perspective), and daylight was a long way off.

As expected, we returned to the scene of the accident about twenty to thirty minutes later. My dad was pretty sure that he had hit what Bobby thought he had (a guy on all fours in a black rubber wetsuit crawling across the road in the dark) and that he would be arrested and sent to prison—or worse.

We got out and looked around and were relieved (in a way) that although we did find some now not-so-fresh blood smears on the pavement, there was no 'body' to be found—no guy in a wetsuit, no big black dog, etcetera—nothing.

Looking around on both sides of the road, we saw that it was kind of muddy and swampy, but not deep enough for a crushed body to sink out of sight. The sun was starting to come up over the horizon when we finally called it quits and went back to my uncle's house. The rest of the trip was without incident, and we didn't run over anything, mysterious or otherwise, on the way home.

My uncle kept an eye on his local newspapers for a few weeks, just in case, but nothing out of the ordinary was ever reported. Years later, my sister's husband, Bobby, ran over a deer with his car in Georgia, and it made a similar mess, although not as bloody. To this day, we have no idea what it was we ran over on the road all those years ago.

CHAPTER 83

THE VOICE IN THE WELL

Once, I heard a voice in the old abandoned well at my grand-mother's house out in the country. Although the well was no longer used, it had supplied my grandma and her family for decades (prior to indoor plumbing).

I knew where the well was and had been warned not to play in or around it. Of course, being a child of eight years old, this only made the well that much more attractive to me! So one thing led to another, and soon enough, in my fantasy world (I had quite the imagination, mind you) the well had become the last outpost with clean water on the prairie, and I was defending it from wild Indians.

I was standing on top of the rotting boards covering the hole (not even realizing the imminent danger this entailed) with a 'rifle' made from a tree branch, fending off the redskins for all I was worth, when suddenly, I heard a voice call out:

"Get down...NOW!"

I leapt off the boards onto the ground and quickly spun this way and that. I expected to see one of my uncles (as the voice had been that of a male), but there was no one in sight...Being in a large cleared-off area, I could see quite a ways, and there was also nowhere anyone could have hidden themselves.

The eerie voice that I heard was talking to ME! So I lit out like a wild savage myself. I was kind of tired of fighting Indians, anyway. I asked around and nobody would let on that they knew anything. I figured someone might have fallen in the well and died, but if they did, I couldn't find anyone that would even admit it, much less talk about it. Beats me!

CHAPTER 84

PHANTOM TRAIN CRASH

An Oneida & Western train crashed off a bridge in a heavily wooded area in middle Tennessee. For years after, it's said that on or near the anniversary of the crash, it continues to replay over and over again. I had heard the story growing up in Jamestown, but I myself had never heard the phantom train, although my grandmother had once. In the early 1980s, I was out in the woods not too far from the tracks one Thanksgiving afternoon. Suddenly, I heard the high, lonesome sound of a steam train off in the distance. Odd thing about that is, there hasn't been a train run through there in at least the last fifty or so years, and the rails have been taken up in most of the area. I knew at once it must be the phantom train, as that's what sprang to mind.

The steam train continued on up through the woods, and about where I believe it would have crossed the river, I heard a terrible crash. It sounded as if the train, trestle and all, had plunged into the river below. Following the crash, I heard some voices, sounded like men yelling, and then the forest fell silent again.

I stayed quiet and never heard another thing. I was stone-cold sober and cannot explain what I heard at all.

CHAPTER 85

YAMACRAW

There's an old mining community in southeastern Kentucky, near Stearns and Whitley City, known as Yamacraw. It's no longer a mining community—in fact, it's no longer anything other than a ghost town (and in more ways than one).

I discovered Yamacraw when I was dating a girl from Whitley City back in the 1980s. Her mother had actually grown up in Yamacraw as a child, which would have been back in the 1930s or so. When the mines closed down, the town went with it, and all that's left now is a few foundations and chimneys —and restless spirits.

We had driven out by the old railroad bridge (teenagers and older in Whitley will know exactly the 'parking' spot I'm talking about!) and left the car for a bit of a walkabout. We followed the railroad bed (the rails and cross ties had long since been removed) back into the woods a couple of miles. It was serene by moonlight, but very creepy as well. It's far enough out in the middle of nowhere that you can't see any lights or hear any traffic or anything off in the distance.

I decided we should venture off the old railbed and see what was in the woods. By the light of the full moon, I had spotted some odd-looking structures off a little ways into the thick vegetation under medium to large-sized trees. (Yamacraw had been abandoned since the late 1950s, and this story takes place in the late 1980s, so it was fairly well returning to wilderness when I was there. Some thirty years on almost now, I'm sure it's even harder going.)

Parts of the structure I had spotted were the concrete pylons from an old coal tipple. The tipple was used to add coal to the trains that once chugged along through these hills. In the moonlight, they looked like some kind of strange monoliths, which reminded me of Stonehenge. Tongue firmly in cheek, I've always referred to them as 'Crawhenge' ever since.

A little farther back, there was the remains of what had once been houses for the coal miners. Small, one- or two-room structures, now nothing but foundations, a chimney here and there, and the odd collapsed rock wall.

I was sitting on a low wall, trying to start a fire with some damp tinder in the remains of an old, decrepit fireplace. Off to my right, I heard a low voice and assumed my then-girlfriend was offering fire-starting tips (she was Cherokee and a lot more well-versed in wood lore than this city boy). However, when I turned around, no one was there. Puzzled somewhat, I continued trying to get the spark to catch, when my girl came walking around from the other side of the ruins (where she had been answering 'nature's call,' I suppose).

Immediately, she began quizzing me about what I had been talking about—according to her, I had been murmuring a mile a minute, but just low enough under my breath that she hadn't been able to make out a word I'd been saying. Very odd indeed, as I had been as silent as a church mouse.

I held my finger up to my lips (my spark had finally caught, and a weak flame was stuttering to life in the old chimney, providing the tiniest bit of light), then leaned in and whispered to her that I hadn't said a word and was inclined to believe we weren't alone out here in the woods.

At first, she later confessed that she thought I was just trying to scare her—after all, we were way out in the middle of absolute nowhere, and a lot of guys my age (at the time) might have used the cover of the dark woods to attempt, shall we say, amorous advances. However, nothing could have been further from the truth. My heart was beating a little fast for sure, but that condition was due to what might be lurking in the woods rather than what was lurking in the sweater my date was wearing.

About the time I was whispering, "I think someone else is out here," we heard low voices again. Plural. Voices...There was more than one somebody out here with us. I immediately grabbed my date by the arm and led her into a darker area—no use giving ourselves away by the glowing (although somewhat pitiful) light of my fire. We crouched down below the crumbling foundation and listened, every nerve on alert.

We eventually heard what sounded like four people—a man, a woman, a small child and a baby—pass by. Odd thing about this, the old foundation was in deep brush. There were decades of leaves, branches, twigs, all manner of stuff under our feet (and presumably the feet of anyone passing by). Even the old railbed was overgrown enough that even the stealthiest of ninjas couldn't have walked it silently...Yet the 'family' (I assume) we heard pass by, very near to our hiding spot, did not make any sounds other than with their voices.

Think about that for a while. Voices. No footsteps. Yep, that was the conclusion we arrived at as well—spirits, ghosts, dead folk. We rose from our hiding spot (my tiny fire had fizzled and gone completely out. I dumped a bottle of Coke on it to be sure), and beat a path back to my car. I haven't been back to those woods since, and I haven't seen the girl in over eleven years.

ABOUT THE AUTHOR

Steve Stockton grew up in the wilds of East Tennessee, but now makes his home in the Pacific Northwest, where he enjoys finding all kinds of new, weird places to seek out. As well as the great outdoors, he also enjoys hearing from his readers. If you have a story you'd like to share for future volumes or would just like to say hello, you can reach him at SteveStockton81@Gmail.com.

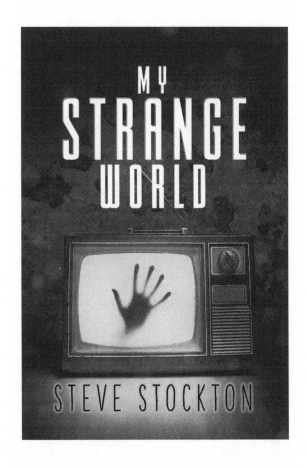

MY STRANGE WORLD

Made in the USA
Columbia, SC
17 February 2022

56405497R00155